Of

Yer Man

And other stories

--------♦--------

Yvonne Heavey

ISBN 978-1-3999-9390-6

Cover design by 100covers.com

Website – yvonneheavey.com

Contents

The Wake of Yer Man

"C'mon, we're late," says Mammy.

"I don't think he's going anywhere Ma, he's dead. What's his name again?" says I.

"It's yer man," Ma says, "you know, yer man."

"So we're going to the wake of yer man?"

"Oh I can't remember his name, he's a good friend of Maura's."

It was going to be my first wake, but I was confused. Was it the removal, Mass or both we were going to after the wake? All I knew was that when someone died they'd be laid out for a couple of days, you'd look at them, then there was loads of drinking and dancing. So Ma sticks on her clean white skirt and smart blazer, tells Da she'll be back later, and I get to go with her to the wake of yer man who I had no notion of. I hoped there might be triangle sandwiches.

"Maura's here," shouts Ma. We blessed ourselves with the holy water as we ran out of the house.

"Don't be gone until you're back," shouts Da.

"We're late," shouts Maura.

"Ah you'd be late to your own funeral," says Mammy in her ever-so-naughty manner.

"The wake's in the house," says Maura. The pair of them lit up cigarettes in the front of the car. "Ah he went quickly in the end, a great age he was," blowing cigarette smoke out of the window.

"I remember the kindness he showed us as kids, but he could turn on ya all the same," says Ma. "Are you going to the removal or the Mass or both after the wake?" This was always a vital question. Even at the grand age of ten I knew the answer to this loaded question depended on a number of factors. How well did you know the family, how far away was the church, will there be a feed and drinks afterwards.

Mammy and Maura were cousins, but sisters at heart, and were well able to chat. Sitting in the back of the car I drifted in and out of their conversation while admiring the fields and boglands of the Midlands. Rain showers then sun, black clouds to clear skies, a constant movie up there.

"Mary is in an awful way, she's not coping at all," says Maura.

"Ah he was 98, Maura, that's some life."

"Yeah, hard all the same. Sure she probably drove him to it," says Maura. The pair of them laughed their heads off. "Jesus, we'd best keep the volume down, we're going to a wake not awakening the dead. We're sending him off to meet St. Peter at the Pearly Gates."

"Are you all right?" Ma turned to me in the back.

"Ma, what do I do?"

"Nothing. You're just coming to pay your respects."

"Sure I'll take this right turn here," says Maura. There was a little slip road that guided us up towards poor auld Jimmy, yer man. Potholes galore and we're shook around like in a washing machine, Mammy and Maura like kids in the front.

"Jesus, Maura, I didn't realise we were your crash test dummies," says Mammy.

With the organs rattled out of us we were pulling up to a grand old farmhouse. Behind some big silver gates were about 20 cars. "Jump out there and open the gate," says Maura to me. It was a squeaky old gate, and it made a haunting shriek as I pushed it open. I'd never been to a wake, so the sound was all too appropriate in my suddenly nervous state. I closed the gate behind Maura's car and followed it over the stony front yard. There was Mary at the door seeing some people off. She was dressed completely in black from head to toe, wiping her eyes. I stared at her as Maura's car parked up and the two of them jumped out.

"Ah, poor Mary," they said, Ma grabbing my hand.

"Ah, Patty, Maura, thank you for coming," said this little woman in black, decrepit, solitary, gentle and sad of voice. "And who are you?" she asked me, "A young Heavey no doubt," kind to me through her pain.

"Polly," I said quietly and shyly. Mary was good-natured but I sensed her broken heart.

"I'll get the kettle on," she said.

"Maura told me the news," says Ma to Mary as she wrapped her arms all around Mary's petite body.

"Come in, come in, you'll catch your death of cold," says Mary, wiping her red raw eyes.

A low murmur of conversation filled the house. We went in the back way through the scullery. There stood two middle-aged women, one washing dishes, the other drying them.

"Hello, dear," they greeted me. They reminded me of the Bingo Bus ladies.

"Will ya get the kettle on, ladies," says Mary, and find some 7Up for the cailín óg."

We all stood in the kitchen hanging on Mary's every word, feeling her gentle pain. "Come on, come on," she says, and we followed her out of the scullery like a row of ants. As a child, following the adults, I didn't feel like I was walking into a sad place.

"He's laid out in the front room," says Mary. We approached the front room through the big kitchen. The kitchen was full of people, a dozen or more chatting about days gone by. A couple of women sat beside the fire, smoke filled the air, and gossip flew around, not many tears in the kitchen anyway. The two tea ladies made their way here and there through the crowded kitchen making newcomers welcome and bidding farewell to those leaving.

There was some craic going on in the corner of the kitchen, no one taking heed of the laughter and divilment going on there. "Ma, why are they laughing at a wake? No one looks sad to me," I said.

"Because we are celebrating Jimmy's life," answered Ma. I didn't understand. We hadn't even seen Jimmy at this stage, laid out in his best.

There were some other kids engrossed in a jigsaw left out for them on a side table out of the way of the adults. I didn't want to get involved in jigsaws. I was in wonderment at being at my first wake, sipping from a warm 7Up and a custard cream in my hand. A table in the middle of the kitchen with the triangle sandwiches. Old farmers' lads sipping the longest cups of tea in history. All the men congregated together, glasses of whiskey in hand.

Fond chat of Jimmy closed the boxes of silence as they gargled down their drinks.

"Sure he was a grand man."

"A great worker."

"Hands of steel."

"Sure if I get to half his age I'll be lucky."

"He's laid out in the front room, Patty," said Maura.

"Will I come with you, Mammy?"

"There's no need. You stay in the kitchen."

They left their drinks on the kitchen table amongst the Benson & Hedges packets. I pulled out a chair at the table, looking at Mary with a silent plea. "Sit there, child," she said. I kept my head down, staring at the non-bubbles in my 7Up.

An auld lad hands me a punt. "That's for you, love." He must have felt sorry for me. I was lost in thought about what Ma was doing. I was glad she didn't bring me as I thought I might have nightmares afterwards.

"You're a young Heavey," says the old farmer.

"I am," I said. The evening was getting on. The people had all paid their respects and there was drunkenness in the air, a combination of smoke and booze. That didn't bother me. Everyone was friendly and I felt safe.

Ma was soon back. "What did you do, Ma? What was he like? Was he scary?"

"No, not at all, very peaceful, lovely man. We kneeled and said a prayer and kissed his forehead."

I'd thought my first wake would be a vale of tears and sorrow, but as the evening wore on it took on a new aspect, and even merriment. The fact that Jimmy had led a full life seemed to mean that a celebration was in order, even in death. Dare I say it was as good as a birthday party. Had it been a young person it would have been different, but this was becoming a jolly sort of event.

I watched and listened to the grown-ups chat away – local gossip, politics, sport, more politics, happenings in the village. Mammy in her magic way creating a wave of laughter amongst her group. Dancing around, she had the personality to light up any room and any wake. People came and went yet still the party continued. Then Mary called everyone to attention.

"Shall we all take the Rosary?" We all moved into the sitting room, huddled into a circle and big Tom Daly took the role of giving out the Rosary with a will. He blasts it out with a mix of machine gun and atomic bomb as if determined to overcome the enemies of God. It was certainly a different approach to how Nancy would say the Rosary.

"Let us now speak with our good Mother!" roars Tom. We all bowed our heads, me kneeling between Ma and Maura. After the recital, the storytelling began. Old Johnny Walsh sat in one corner surrounded by big-eared listeners while another old dear recounted her story in another corner. The evening was long, but the stories kept everyone awake, Jimmy this and Jimmy that, and then when the stock of Jimmy stories was exhausted, other stories were told.

Then suddenly a hush descended as Mary stood to attention. "Sshhhhh." Respect for Mary whose husband had passed. And in the quiet seconds a tune arose, Mary was belting out a song that Jimmy loved. She sang her heart out and then we all joined in. "From a distance the world looks blue and green..." Tears fell, but not tears of sadness. Tears for a life well spent. A good Rosary and a good song was the perfect opportunity for people to politely drift back into the kitchen. The two ladies were still washing up, making tea, pouring drinks. It was almost midnight by now and a few more people had left. I was terribly excited to be allowed to still be hanging out this late, but by now I was fighting back the tiredness.

I noticed new things happening in the kitchen. The drunker people got, the more games were being played. Even Mary began to join in – riddles, tongue-twisters, even a bit of wrestling between big Tom Daly and Sean Fitzpatrick. "Tom, do you think we need to be heading home?" says Maura. "Is wrestling not a bit disrespectful?"

"Will ya stop. A wake's an institution of our ancestors and to have a bit of fun. Sure wouldn't Jimmy be the first to join in?"

Way past midnight, drinks still being offered. Card playing, riddling, and rhyming, strongman contests between the old farmers, mocking and taunting at the outcomes, mischief making. One thing I learnt that day is that if an Irish person had lived a long and useful life then their wake was an exciting place to be. Big Tom Daly, bald with a big belly, lies over the kitchen table. Barry O'Shea, about the same size, gets together with his brother Sean and heaves Tom's legs up so that he's now lying completely on the table. By this stage even Mary was crying with laughter. Someone put a Guinness bottle in Tom's hand, and we all gathered around the body and sang, "Show me the way to go home."

"This is the way Jimmy would have wanted the wake to end," shouts Mary.

Tinkers Hill

The dampness of the morning soaked my shoes, seeping into my socks as I sprinted to catch up with Da, my breaths shallow and quick in the crisp air. “Da, wait up,” I called, beaming with pride as I pulled on my schoolbag, which felt as empty as our fridge. “Da, I’ve emptied out all my schoolbooks, so loads of room for the tins,” I said, practically bouncing on my toes just to glimpse his face hidden way up in the rainclouds of his blazer jacket.

“Good girl,” Da grinned, the rain dripping off his nose, “sure, we only need a few dozen, that’ll tide us over and I’ll get you something nice in Bradley’s tomorrow for all your hard work. You’re a great girl,” he winked. “Oh, pull that over your head,” he said, plopping a black woolly hat on my head.

I glanced up at him, my hat drooping like a soggy cake. “Thanks, Da, do you not have one?”

“That’s mine, you have it, Das don’t get wet,” he said while the raindrops pelted his face. I loved the smell, a smell of Da, cold turf fires and damp and Old Spice. We crossed over the road, and Da and I stood at the thumbing stop just across the road from the Derrygreenagh Park sign. I might as well have had no shoes on with splashes of muck all over my grey school socks and I could feel raindrops like cold little kisses plopping on my woolly hat. Da, his jacket collar turned up against the wind, gave me a wink. "Sure, we're a right pair aren't we," he cackled.

Every car that passed was a blur of hope that skidded away as fast as the rain poured. Da stuck his thumb out, his big hand steady as an old oak, while my little thumb wobbled like a new leaf. I felt another rumble in my tummy. I silently prayed and made a few bargains with God if he'd let the next car stop. "God, you see, I have been a pretty good girl this week. I helped Ma and Da with giving them a few pounds of my babysitting money, and I said the Novena every night before lights out. Listen, God, if you do me this favour I will owe you one, promise." My internal chat made me forget about the rumbling tummy.

"Are ya alright?" says Da, pulling me in a bit closer to shade off some rain, "there'll be one stopping soon," he said.

"Da, let's pass the time," I said with a chill along my spine, a raindrop making its way down my neck. "Let's play I Spy." But it was tough with everything all different shades of rain. "I spy with my little eye, something beginning with..." and just as I squinted hard to see something, anything, Da laughs and says, "Wet!"

Then God kept his side of the bargain: a miracle, a car pulled over. It was old Mrs Claffey from Tyrrellspass. The back of her Cortina was stuffed with bags of knitting and a dog named Seamus, who was the only dog I knew with eyebrows like a cartoon, but there was room for the two of us. "Jump in, craturs, can't have ye swimming to Mullingar!" she laughed. We squished into the back seat, and off we went, to the sound of *All God's Creatures got a Place in the Choir* coming from the radio. Mrs Claffey was the deeply religious sort that did the holy hour each Sunday and had a shrine to Holy God draped on the dashboard and rear-view mirror, all rosary beads and Catholic saints' bobbleheads nodding in silent assent. She wore big round glasses that made her eyes look like they were about to break a massive secret that only you were lucky enough to be told.

Da leaned in, his voice tickling my ear, and held my thumb in his damp hand. "Thank ye, little thumb," he whispered into my thumb, "you've saved the day." I felt my cheeks glow though my socks were soggy.

As the car bumped along and Seamus snored, I watched the raindrops race each other along the window. Mrs Claffey smiled at me in the mirror, keeping the rest of her attention on the lurching pot-holed Mullingar road. The car was her church altar, her shrine to Baby Jesus, and as the opening notes of her favourite hymn floated from the radio, she began singing along, her voice slightly off-tune but a sincere instrument of her faith. It was clear that Mrs Claffey felt each word deeply, her voice rising and falling with the pretty melody.

Between verses she'd have a little chat with us. "Isn't it just a blessing how the auld daisies are blooming early this year? Hallelujah!"

"Oh it is, grand to see the flowers blooming," says Da as if he meant it. The conversation stopped there, taken over by a rant about a grocery list, a reminder to call her sister, and then the heights of a particularly rousing Amen, all delivered in one breathless blur. I wondered if she had any sweets in the car.

We were nearly at the greyhound racetrack. Mrs Claffey's finger reached out to the radio, the volume of the holy hymns descending into a quiet lull. She glanced over her shoulder. "Oh, Jim, where will I drop you and the young one?" Her voice carried the unmistakable timbre of a slightly intrusive concern.

Da shuffled in his seat, his hands clasping in a silent show of appreciation. "Thanks a million, Mrs

Claffey, anywhere that suits you," he said. "We're very grateful."

"Thanks a million," I echoed. It was an awkward chorus, our gratitude stuck on repeat.

"Ah, Jim, I don't mind. I would pull up anywhere," Mrs Claffey assured us, her voice cutting through the silence left by the now muted hymns. Her eyes held ours in the rear-view mirror for one second longer than was needed.

We exchanged a quick glance, Da and I, sharing the silent agreement to keep our destination, St. Vincent de Paul, our secret. "Mount Street would be grand," Da let out, finally settling on a place. Mount Street was grand, but it was four streets' walk from where we were heading.

"Are ya sure?" Mrs Claffey turned her body to face us entirely, the concern in her eyes scanning our faces for any trace of hesitation.

"That would be perfect," Da assured her with a firm nod.

I shifted in my seat, grimacing at the sensation of pointed metal against my flesh. The tin opener had wedged itself firmly in the back pocket of my jeans. With each bump and turn along the road, the jagged implement embedded itself deeper into my backside. I had shoved it into my back pocket for later and hadn't even noticed its presence as we'd made our way down the auld Mullingar road. My bum ached, but the warmth in Mrs Claffey's car and the deliverance it offered prevailed. "Thanks a million again, thanks," says Da and I in harmony, as we stood on the side of the street. Mrs Claffey pulled away, beeping her horn as if she was attending a wedding. We waved back at her until she turned the corner.

The rain had eased but the air was damp. We were damp. I hated anything damp. Da and I, squelching feet after feet, proceeded down Mount Street. The town was barely awake, its main thoroughfare a grey, sleepy river of tired faces, but the shop windows were cosy frames of light and colour. We could see in the distance the blue Georgian building of St. Vincent de Paul's to which we had made many visits. We approached by the side door, not the front entrance, to avoid detection. With the Mrs Claffeys of this world one could never be too careful. The ache in my tummy intensified as the prospect of being fed grew closer. I could taste the first bite even before I made it to the door. I checked my back pocket; the tin opener was still there. Da pressed the bell, its ding-a-ling jingle announcing the enormous feast on the other side. Once inside it was like being in Granny's house, all lavender and the scent of clean. I could see a shadow coming to the door. "Aha, what's this we have here?" said Kathleen McDowell, looking at me, her face crumpled like my copy books for homework. She wore a cardigan that held every colour of the rainbow and carried the look of kindly attentiveness that always greeted us when we came to St. Vincent's, a look that I had glimpsed in the Cortina. I hated that look, but the way my tummy was feeling every look or gesture annoyed me. "You're like two wet cats, get into the hallway here and heat yerselves up."

We stood in the orange-tiled hallway and Dad gave her a smile that didn't quite reach his eyes. "Hi, Kathleen. We wondered, you wouldn't happen to have a bit of food to tide us over?"

"Of course, Jim," Kathleen nodded, bustling around the counter. "We've got some bread, cheese, and a few bits and ends and lots of the usual corned beef, will that do?"

"That's more than enough. We're off to Rochfortbridge, you see, without our car," said Da and he gestured me to place our bags on the counter. Despite our hunger we were steeped in manners. I grinned, showing all my teeth, maybe even the ones at the back. "Thanks so much, Kathleen," Da said, his eyes on Kathleen's precise loading of the Libby's tinned corned beef into my school bag.

Kathleen clicked her tongue, saying, "Rochfortbridge, is it?" as she assessed the tins to squeeze more of them in. The job was taking ages, and the rumbling in my belly would have been audible only for Kathleen's rustling. Would she ever stop? All I kept thinking was I could make a cheese sandwich right in front of her; two grabs of bread and a chunk of cheese would do it.

"We're like mules!" I laughed to Da.

Kathleen asked if we wanted to stay for a cup of tea, but Da said we had to get back to the others at home, so she walked us to the door.

"Good luck, good luck, Kathleen, thanks a million. Hopefully won't be seeing us too soon!" shouts Da, pulling down the damp woolly hat on my head so it covered my eyes.

"Thanks, Mrs McDowell," I said, in a giggly muffled voice from under the hat.

The brown door closed behind us. "C'mon, let's get outta here."

We played dodge with the puddles. They had turned the colour of a cup of Lloyd's tea, creamy and strong. Each step made a squelching noise, but this time the discomfort couldn't dampen my spirits. After all, I had the tin opener in my pocket and a bag full of corned beef. Even before I left Mrs McDowell's thoughtful gaze I was plotting how I could open a tin on my way home without annoying

Da. I had my school bag of corned treasure. “Are we going up Tinkers Hill, Da?” I was hoping he’d say we would loop around it, as it was more like a mountain than a hill.

“Yeah, it’ll be a shortcut, you’ll be grand.”

“Ah, Da!” I said with a moan. The hill always seemed to go on forever, and I didn’t want to be stopping halfway up on a slant opening my corned beef. My breath hitched in bursts as I scrambled up the hill, three strides to Da’s lanky one. The foretaste of that corned beef kept my speed up, despite the creeping soreness in my legs. Da leant forward as he walked, no messing or lingering. He was intent on finishing our mission. He stretched further ahead of me, and the tin opener was in my right hand as I reached back with my left under the flap of the school satchel for the first tinned offering. After a rapid darting manoeuvre, a tin of corned beef now nestled in my cupped palm. My eyes flicked to Da’s receding figure as I waged war on the tin. It took three efforts for the cutting wheel to catch on the edge before I remembered the tin had its own key. The damp made the operation nearly impossible as I removed the key from its hold and turned it around. With the first twist, the curled tin revealed its pink fleshy sacrament. I twisted and twisted till the entire bottom of the can had opened. My life itself seemed to hang on the salted pink beef. Greed got the better of me, and I nipped one of my fingers on a serrated edge as I wrested the meat into my hands. I grabbed a chunk and lodged the remains of the rectangle in my pocket, replacing the empty tin and the opener back in the satchel.

"What you at?" Da played the seer unseeing, the sparkle in his eye belying his ignorance. It was our silent treaty.

"Grand, Da," I said, the words half-muffled as a chunk of corned beef lodged stubborn in my throat. I battled it down as he approached. "Da, want a slice?" My right hand, a mix of raw blue and blistering red, held a hunk of hearty beef.

He snatched it with a chuckle. "Jesus, you've no patience," he laughed. And so we climbed the hill, rain drizzling on my sodden hat, hardly a shield against the sky's teary eyes. Our path was etched with straining and chewing. "Shall we have a go at another tin?" Da said, a scheming gleam in his eye.

"We will, Da, we will," I said, and we smiled together, and the rain stopped falling and even Tinkers Hill was already behind us.

The Magic Bicycle

When Mammy was a child she wrote a story called The Magic Bicycle and was awarded some shillings from the Bishop of Meath. Let me tell you how it all happened.

You see, my grandmother, Mary Ellen, fell for a man who would be my granddad. But there was a twist. Grandad was already married. Back in 1950's Catholic Ireland, if you were unmarried and expecting a baby, it usually meant a one-way ticket to a nunnery. But Mary Ellen's mother and her Uncle Jim spared her that fate. The week before her First Communion, Mary Ellen passed away and Mammy then went to live with her mother's sister, who had two daughters, Maura and Celie. Mammy grew up with Maura and Celie as her sisters and they all attended Castlejordan primary school.

Mammy's mother passed when she was only seven. It was hard but somehow, she always found a way to keep smiling, especially when she wrote. She loved telling stories.

The prize-winning story is lost now, but my Aunt Celie remembers the time it was read aloud in front of the whole school. Ma was in fifth or sixth class, Maura was a year above her, and Celie was another year down. Celie says the story was about a dream and a bicycle, but she can't remember the details.

It was said that Mammy's Da bought her a blue and red bicycle with tassels on the side. It was 23 punt.

I often wondered about that prize-winning story. I asked Mammy many times to re-tell it. She'd just change the subject but, every now and then, she would mention it out of the blue, not the story she wrote but the actual bicycle, as if it was a living thing.

Mammy loved pointing out the stars - the Plough, Little Bear, the Pole Star. She'd say the bike took her to the Moon and back. I'd think about where else it might have taken her. Distant galaxies? A Black Hole? Did she ride it when she was happy or sad, maybe to escape the real world. How did the magic work? Did Mammy whisper a magic word like "Abracadabra!"? I imagined the bike glowing, coming alive, and zooming off like a rocket! So many questions.

Maybe Mammy used the bicycle to visit her father, who fell down a well. Or perhaps it took her back to the days when her mother Mary Ellen, who died so young, was still alive.

I'd love to hear her prize-winning story of the Magic Bicycle. But maybe I'm meant to write my own version, a fragment of memories from a story lost long ago. One that connects us, mother and daughter, on our magic bikes, journeying through galaxies and life.

I think even Mammy might have forgotten she was once young, after everything she'd been through. The Magic Bicycle reclaimed the past and opened a portal to the dearly departed.

One day, I'll read Mammy's story, the one she wrote so many years ago. Don't ask me when or where; I just know I will. For now, knowing that her story was good enough for the Bishop of Meath is good enough for me.

Turf Bags and the Big Snow

"The year Baby Dumps was born," Mammy said as she tugged the kitchen curtain open, "the snow was piled so high it swallowed the clothesline. The clothes looked they were frozen in time, like the Ice Age had come again, not a neighbour in sight for days."

The snow pattered the glass, a soft steady thunk of snowflakes. "Ah sure, this storm looks just as bad as the last," said Mammy, staring out at our half-buried garden.

We squashed ourselves onto the old couch, barely woken, glued to the scene outside the window. The flickering shadows from the open range made our height charts on the wall under the Sacred Heart picture dance like jumping spirits. Micheal's was highest with his six-foot mark, while the rest of ours made steps below his, even down to Bingo Heavey's tiny dog mark. Da stood by the range fire with his blue sleeves rolled up, shoving old boots and shoes into the flames. The turf and briquettes were all gone, the roads were buried, and outside, the wind continued to howl.

I wanted to feel the storm's gentle power against my skin, but inside, behind the window, was where we felt safe. Outside was Jack Frost, probably best friends with the storm, like waves are to the sea. Jack Frost had caught me once. Ma was at the hospital collecting Baby Dumps and Da let me play outside. I had just my Communion socks on my hands trying to keep my red fingers warm. I built half a snowman before Jack Frost pounced.

"If you leave your fingers in the snow too long, he'll get you, didn't I tell you," Da told me as he ran the warm water tap over my frost-bitten hand. Jack Frost was invisible like Holy God, but unkind. He did mean things to kids, making them slip on the gravel and turning their fingers purple. I wondered whether he might be hiding in the storm, waiting for his next chance to pounce.

"Can we go out?" asked Aine.

"Not yet," I said, shaking my head. "Jack Frost is hiding out there."

"Will ya give it up and settle down?" Liam grumbled, eyes fixed on the TV. "We're trying to watch the Everton game." Ma always joked that if two ants were playing with a crumb, we'd have it on the telly. It was either football, golf, Nigel Mansell in F1 races (Ma loved Nigel), or snooker.

"Can we watch something else?" Caroline whined.

"The game's nearly over," Micheal snapped, eyes never leaving the screen.

Seamus, the second oldest brother, was buried in a book about world wars. He knew everything about cars, machines, wars, politics.

Finally, after absorbing the last of the old boots, the range started to give out heat as the snowstorm raged outside. Siobhan sat, brushing her long, thick, beautiful red hair. She was the Irish dancer in the house, the oldest sister, and I was sure she had already kissed a boy. I dreamed of kissing boys but hadn't gotten the chance. So, every now and then, I would practice on the mirror. Shifting the mirror just right, I'd kiss my reflection.

The boys had their eyes glued to the telly. Even if a tornado hit, they wouldn't notice.

"Will ya just stick it in the fecking net!" Micheal fumed.

Da chopped onions in the scullery, and Mammy, peeling a big bag of spuds sat in her armchair with a kitchen knife. Every now and then, Daddy would try to tickle Mammy. "Get off me, Jim, will ya leave me alone!" Mammy shooed him away but smiled all the same.

"Ah sure, ya love a little cuddle," Da teased from the kitchen, tossing a grin her way.

"It's a goal!"

The lads shot up from their seats with a chorus of screams. The whole house felt like it jumped up with them. Da, just about to burn another Doc Marten boot, flung it instead. It sailed across the room, hurtling into the Sacred Heart picture on the wall. At the same time, there was a bang on the door. Caroline ran to the door first. The storm was wild, howling through the gaps in the windows. She opened the door, and the wind nearly pulled her out. She screamed, "Da, someone's left a bale of briquettes outside!"

"Jaysus, who would put them out in that weather?" Da came rushing, his eyes bloodshot from peeling the onions. "Get in, get in!" he said to Caroline. We all followed as Da grabbed the bale, wrestling with it against the gale. "Thanks be to God," he said, looking up at the saintly picture hanging by the door. "Sure, you always answer our prayers, Padre Pio." Da snipped the orange wire coiled round the briquettes. There were little patches of snow on some of the briquettes, a taste of what was in store for us. "It had to be Old Bill Cooney who delivered them. He'd be out in all sorts of weather, even these days."

Ma, sitting in her usual spot, was engrossed in peeling spuds. "Those footprints are too big to be Old Bill's," she said, flicking back the kitchen curtain. "Must've been size 12 feet and had a very distinctive diamond shape on the track in the snow on the way up to the house. Ah, sure maybe it was Bigfoot!" Ma chuckled. "Ah well," she sighed, her voice full of relief, "I don't care if it was John the Baptist himself that left them at the door. We can hold back on the old boots now, Jim."

She stood up, her chair creaking softly, and lifted the bucket of spuds. "Be a good girl and wash these," she instructed, handing me the bucket. I dragged it into the scullery, my eyes looking under the net of the frosted window. Snow covered the little Fiat out front, transforming it into a solid, windowless block. With a twist of the tap, ice cold water gushed out, and I plunged the spuds under, scrubbing away the dirt.

The game over, the lads had vanished up to the landing to play snooker. At last, the living room was ours. I gave the spuds one last rapid rinse and then joined the sisters on the couch. We pressed the button on the telly flipping to RTÉ. We made it just in time, as *Skippy the Bush Kangaroo* flickered on the screen. "Can we get a kangaroo?" Aine enquired, as if the house had an ounce of space for a jumping animal from Australia. Sure we already had Bobby Gilson's son Bingo Heavey, the family dog.

"No kangaroos in Ireland," Tracey said, matter of fact, as we huddled on the couch, the storm outside forgotten for a second. We were spellbound by the Outback and Skippy's heroics. On the telly, a park scene unfolded. A lady let go of her pram, and it was rolling dangerously close to the water.

"No, no, Skippy, where are you?" Caroline yelled. I felt my own terror rising, hands over my mouth. The baby was mere inches from the edge.

And just like that, it happened. The screen fizzed, a final whoosh, and then—nothing. Pitch black. TV blank. All house lights gone. "Ah, Jaysus! Did the storm knock the electrics off too?" I wondered aloud.

"No," Ma said, "I think the meter's run dry."

"Mammy, have ya got a 50 pence on ya?" says Da.

"Check my auld bag behind the door," Ma replied. "Should be a couple of coins rattling at the bottom of it."

Da flicked his lighter and went into the hallway to feed the meter. He found the 50p in Ma's handbag and fiddled with the ESB box. Da was a wizard with that old meter, always knowing how to make the budget stretch. Even the Trocaire box wasn't safe from the odd raid from time to time. And then, flick! The lights came back to life, and the telly was back but Skippy had finished his saviour scene. Outside the snow slowed to a gentle flurry and the wind had lessened.

"Is it my turn on the radio now?" Da asked, tuning the radio. *Tie a Yellow Ribbon Round the Old Oak Tree* was playing softly. "Turn down that telly! I love this tune," Da said, his voice drowning in the mix of television chatter, laughter, and arguments.

"Turn it down, turn it down, Jim!" Mammy lifted the net curtain, just enough for a secret peek. "Now there's old Mrs O'Loony Bin out there, otherwise known as Mrs Shanigan," Mammy's voice took on a dramatic flair. "Tiny little thing, no taller than my leg, with hair wild like a red bush on fire." Mrs O'Loony Bin was slithering down the sidewalk in her dressing gown and clunky boots, snow flying up with each step. The storm was calmer now and the people of Derrygreenagh began to make their appearance.

"What the Nora is she wearing?" Mammy laughed.

Other neighbours now made their appearance, creeping out of their homes as if from a winter hibernation. They shovelled their doorsteps, and shook the white powder off the bin lids, marvelling at the white magic that had transformed our estate. We began thinking of an escape ourselves. Movement at last after a morning of rapture, watching the snowfall from the vantage of the couch.

"What's in the stew, Da?" Caroline enquired.

"Denny's sausages, black pudding, carrots and full onion heads," Da said, adding, "and a cow's big, fat tongue!" A cow's tongue? Had the world gone mad! First a snowstorm out of the North Pole, and now cows' tongues.

"Ah sure that's only for your mother, not as if she doesn't have enough of a gob already on her."

"Go away outta that," says Ma. "Sure there's enough dung running off your tongue."

I moved back to the window, gazing out onto the white wilderness outside. Snowflakes bounced into each other in the tiny garden, settling on my blue tricycle in the garden. I recalled Auntie Pauline saying a snowflake is one of God's most fragile creatures but look what they can do when they stick together. I watched the snowflakes falling. Little by little, like ants gathering together, the snow started to cover the tricycle. Before long it was a white statue, disappearing into another world. The snow had not completely stuck as, in the distance, we could still see one or two green patches. Surely we needed a white world for the magic of Egan's Field to come to life?

"Da, look! The Bollard twins and Dunnes are already out, building castles and everything!" I shouted.

"Aye, sure the stew's almost ready, get this into you first and then we can get on," he said.

"But Da," I pleaded. "The snow won't wait! We can eat when we come back. We need to get to Egan's Field before it turns to slush, there'll be every kid and their dog up there and the snow only stays good for a while."

"Fine, fine, go on then, but make sure ya stay warm."

"Right I'll go and test it first, Da!" I shouted. Still in my pyjamas I stuck on my school shoes as they were waterproof, my favourite Dubarry ones handed down from Alice Markey and the English cousins. I grabbed Micheal's overcoat and opened the back door by the coal hole. An arctic breeze flew past me into the hall. The cold stung my cheeks as I stepped out. The sisters hung back, shivering on the doorstep. A velvet white blanket covered the trees in the forest beyond our little garden. I was amazed at how quiet it was. The only sound I could hear was my Dubarrys crunching the snow beneath. The air was fresh and clean as I walked to the end of the garden and into the field. Beyond the rooftops, I could hear cries and shouts as the Derrygreenagh kids hurled snowballs in the circle.

The spell didn't last long. Da calling me in, screaming that I'd catch my death and what in the name of sweet Mary was I thinking. I retraced each squeaky step, determined not to damage the white padded perfection of the garden, and made my way in through the back door with the swirling flakes following me in. "Now all of ye upstairs and be dressed, quick enough."

All four of the sisters, less Siobhan, scrambled upstairs to get ready. Plastic bags over our feet then socks over them, then tight or too loose trainers. Leggings or tights under trousers. There weren't enough gloves to go round so the younger ones had socks as mittens. Woolly hats to top everything off and we were ready for our trip. Over to the hills behind the McNamaras and Fordes to the field of Farmer Egan.

"Right, grab the turf bags!" Da ordered, tossing some from the press.

"You gotta keep an eye on Aine. Don't take your eyes off her for one second," Ma cautioned.

Da opened the door, dislodging a snowdrift and exposing the warmth of the home to the frozen outside. The Derrygreenagh ring of houses was a hive of cautious movement. The older ones inching gingerly along the pavement, arm in arm, the young ones in the circle building the first of many snowmen. Even the air felt alive, filled with the mingled scents of turf smoke and winter. Snowflakes drifted down from the sky, as if blessing our adventure to the land of Egan's Field, a snowy trek beyond the Derrygreenagh edges. The green stretched out before us, a frosty blanket, pristine and quiet except for the crunch of our runners on the snow.

Just then, Mrs Bollard's voice cut through the air. "Jim, would you look at our old oven? I think it went in the storm," she shouted, one hand gripping her overcoat lapels tight while the other tried to keep her twin grandsons from pelting each other with snowballs. Da nodded an 'aye' as he waddled down towards the arch entrance by the Derrygreenagh circle. We could already hear the distant sounds of Egan's Field – children's screeches and whoops of delight. I could see in my mind's eye the huge hilltop and the children trudging their way up to it, dragging turf bags and giggling with the sheer amazement of what awaited them on the summit, maybe a quarter of a mile from top to bottom. Trudging, skipping and slipping behind Da we were about to escape the park.

"Are ye alright, girls?" Da asked, glancing back over his shoulder. "Be careful of the black ice."

No sooner had he spoken than Caroline slipped, pulling the rest of us down like dominoes.

"Caroline, why didn't you let go? Just let go if you're gonna fall," I yelled, frustration melting into giggles as we all lay sprawled in the snow.

And then, as if summoned by some unseen signal, they appeared. The dogs of Derrygreenagh. Mutt Fennelly and his gang stood there in a perfect line, a canine mafia, their curious eyes locked on us. I could see their noses twitching, catching scents, it was like they were deciding which of us was likely to be the tastiest cut. I stopped with Tracey and the others in the middle of the Green, our breath misting in the cold air. I stared at the ground, willing the gangster dogs to lose interest, but you could feel Mutt's eyes. He was the boss, the capo of the crew don't you know it! He had a watchful, malevolent look on him, waiting for the first sign of fear. Behind him, Spot Bollard, Rover Graham, Sparky Cully, and Charlie Bollard formed a loyal posse, their tails wagging together. The dogs of Derrygreenagh bore the surnames of their owners and they owned the neighbourhood. No one could pass them by without their say-so.

Then, just as it seemed they might pounce, they started. A chorus of barks, rising and falling, led by Mutt's own deep voice. Each bark was a note in their wild orchestra, with Mutt as the maestro, his head held high. "Just let them bark. Don't look scared and keep moving calmly. They'll lose interest," Da's advice was hard to follow when it was icy underfoot and the snow swiftly falling.

Mutt, perhaps satisfied with his performance, gave us one last, withering glance. He strutted off, the pack trailing obediently.

Da muttered under his breath, "He really thinks he rules this place, that Mutt Fennelly one." And maybe, in his own way, he did.

When we finally reached Egan's big hill, my eyes popped wide open. There were kids and adults everywhere, swooshing down the mountain like we were in Switzerland! A few of the grown-ups had taken charge, shaping the snow into a starting position. We joined the orderly line of children waiting excitedly for our turn, my sisters behind me which was only fair. Some of our friends were further along and we waved to them. As we edged forward a touch of blue sky appeared, a little light which threw a splash of gold on our snowy adventure. We shuffled up the hill, dragging our turf bags behind us. The hill was packed, everyone shoving to get to the top. Then suddenly it was my turn. I concentrated on the task in hand, sitting on my turf bag, the slope set out below, well marked by the previous riders.

"Fast or slow?" Da asked.

"Fast, fast!" I shouted.

"Hold on to the corners!" instructed Da. I held as hard as I could given the limitations of my socked hands.

"Ready, steady, Go!" shouted Da and the girls, giving me a big push off the launchpad. Off I went flying, mouth open, snow and ice flying into my red raw face. The sensation was electric, as I sped faster than a speeding car. And, like those before me, I screamed. And then as quickly as it began I came to a halt in the slushy stuff at the bottom. I had to pinch myself at the thought of doing it all over again, and again, and again, as I joined the others in the long climb back up Egan's hill. The snow began falling again and I tugged Baby Dumps along with me, her turf bag trailing behind her.

Novena

In Rochfortbridge within the main village lies the chapel, the Church of the Immaculate Conception. It can hold up to 200 souls but that morning the chapel held just me, the darkness and the statues to its stone bosom.

It was late in the month of June 1996, an unusually hot day by Irish summer standards. I was on my own in the chapel, 14 years of fear among the finest statues of Jesus, Mary, all the angels, saints, shrines and Stations of the Cross.

As a child I was afraid of my own shadow so the quietness of the church with only my head voice for company made me speak to God in a rather quick manner. I had that sickness of constant anxiety as I entered the chapel alone. It had only been a few weeks since He took him, and no one knew of my silent plea. My belief in Christ and all the saints was so strong that I believed if I prayed for what I really wanted it would plop right down in front of me. Yet that belief was also fear, the fear of it actually coming to pass and the fear of it not, mixed with the fear of the statues coming to life with their strange Mona Lisa smiles.

The chapel felt different that day, like it was whispering secrets just to me. Saint Joseph held out flowers, looking like he wanted to pass me one, a silent companion. The statues' faces were all so kind. Were these statues trying to win me over with their soft smiles? Each Station of the Cross seemed to tell a story, a tale written just for me.

I lingered at the back, pretending to be interested in the leaflets and prayer books for sale. There were requests to spare a little for the Young Priests' Society, the missionaries, the saints - sure every saint was looking for a spare punt. Prayers for the blind, the deaf, the lonely, the sad, the lost souls, the found souls, money for the orphans, the angels, the alcoholics, Virgin Mary, you name it there was either a prayer request or a plea for a few shillings. But what about a prayer for the resurrection of Da Heavey of Rochfortbridge, father of nine and a Royal County supporter? Pope Francis always gets mentioned in these prayers. Sure, Pope Francis is lovely, but so was Da. My Da.

Da's memory came to me in sudden flashes, bits of kindness jolting around inside my head. There I was, sprinting across the football field in oversized boots, Liam's boots, flopping awkwardly with each step. My feet filled barely half of them, and the Dublin team was playing rough. I couldn't keep up, the pain from the boots was unbearable. I kept tripping.

But then, at half time, there was Da on the sideline, holding a shoebox. He shouted, "Got you a new pair!" The price tag on the box said 30 punts, more than a quarter of Da's weekly pay. The new boots had luminous sides, and my heart soared. I was over the moon!

I remember the long walk to St Vincent's with Da, his voice singing *Beautiful Meath*: *Oh, beautiful Meath, you've got all that I need, your rivers they flow with delight.* He was always strides ahead of me, turning over his shoulder as he sang and shouting to me to catch up.

Other times he would say something powerful with meaning, but he never explained what he meant. "You know you're a great girl; don't ever sell yourself short," he would say, his hand tousling my bowl-cut hair. "Stay on the right side of the man above."

"What do you mean, Da?"

Da paused. "God is within you and without you, sure he's everywhere."

As I prayed in the empty cathedral, I saw our bingo trips and felt the crunch of pink bon-bons he'd bought me on the way to Moate. I remembered how he'd always win at our walking races, and how I'd bug him about dyeing his hair, just once. Who will help me carry bags from Bradley's, chat about the ladies' football, or let me show off my art and poems? Who'll get me a Moro bar and a can of Cidona on a Friday? Who'll fix my schoolbooks and meet me after work at O'Meara's and make me stew and drop off my sandwiches at lunch and teach me the things only he knew?

I flitted through the pile of leaflets by the porch, picking up a small prayer booklet, its bold letters promising *Ask and You Shall Receive*, priced 50p. Thinking it wouldn't hurt to try, I picked up the leaflet and dropped a 50p piece into the brown box. I continued down the aisle.

"Okay, God," I whispered in my mind. "I've asked. When will I receive?"

In front of the transept to the right was a set of stained-glass windows. The tiny panes danced with colours - emerald, sapphire, and ruby, framing the faces of gentle angels. Larger panes held solemn figures of Christ and the Apostles, their forms calm against the shimmering, intricate lace-like details. Farther up, balcony windows illustrated scenes from the Gospel according to Matthew, vibrant with hues of red and blue. The rich colours and detailed glasswork seemed to pulse with life, an unspoken promise in every glint and shadow.

I reached the top of the aisle and opened the prayer book, my mind a whirl of confusion. Why would God help me of all people? Sure he's not going to lift a finger for someone like me. Guilt washed over me as I remembered the nights spent with a made-up Ouija board, the Scrabble tiles, and the confirmation chains at Mrs Gunning's house.

"Sorry God, and sorry for saying the Our Father backwards in a mirror and lighting candles. I know it was black magic, but my friends made me do it and we got scared and we didn't finish it anyways."

As the memories replayed themselves, I felt even more lost. I sighed deeply, hoping for some divine sign.

I remembered Daddy's stories, like the time he and Uncle Liam built a bridge in Ballinabrackey over the frozen river when they were just ten. They were so proud when it stood tall through the seasons and years. But when we found it decades later on the way to Granny's it was a tiny thing, just two logs stuck in the ooze and tied together by rope. Uncle Pat was his best friend, but he went to England when he turned 29. Years later, Daddy got a letter. Uncle Pat had been hit by a car in London. Maybe it happened on a bridge. Daddy never talked about it after that.

The sun shone a superb ray through the stained glass and as I scrunched up my green eyes, the red and blue radared off my whole being. It felt as if hands were lifting my arms and floating me upwards. I thumbed to the first page and, with the purple shine upon it, started to read a Novena.

I took a deep breath, feeling the warmth of the sunlight mix with the chill in my heart. This was it. The first step. Nine days, nine prayers. A promise is a promise, God.

“Dear God, it’s me. I’m saying this prayer. The Novena. Nancy said you grant wishes if you hear it nine times. Well, it was Father’s Day when you took Da. Why’d you have to do that? So, please, can you bring him back, just for a day? Ok I will write it in here so you know I am actually saying it. God, I have to go home soon. Ma’s so sad, we all are, and I want to check on her before everyone arrives for the memorial mass. Even Bingo Heavey’s sad, not barking or chewing the sofa. Tracey said he’s gone to the end of the garden and all he does is make a whining sound. One more thing—could you please make the church less scary next time? The statues seem to stare at me, and it’s like they’re about to jump out. If you bring Da back I won’t ask for anything else. We don’t need more money or a bigger house. I just want Da.”

Closing the leaflet, I shuffled down the aisle. I’d promised myself to finish the Novena, but those statues with their stoney eyes made me afraid. I’d kept watching them, just in case they decided to move. If they did, I'd have to bolt it before they could grab me. I hate things sneaking up on me.

At the end of the aisle, I whispered, "Hear my prayer, God. Amen." I bowed my head and brushed my cheeks and stepped out into the scorching sun.

10/1 at Leopardstown

"Can you tell me the time, the correct time!" he says, pushing past us. Sure, time was time and what other time would I tell him but the correct time, I thought. There was a ciggie hanging from his mouth where his teeth should've been. Da and I stood in the warmth of the bookies, where the rustle of paper and the shouting of odds was its own sort of song. It was Friday, Da's social payout day and we felt flush, a few shillings jingling together in our pockets.

"Two oh five," I said to the man.

"Grand, grand. I'll be backing me luck at Punchestown," he muttered through a haze of fag smoke. The man took his place in front of the tellies, eyes squinting at the flickering horses. His hair, long and stringy, was slicked back with a sheen of Brylcreem. A stale, sour odour of last night's booze clung to him. He shifted in his seat, adjusting his dirty coat and brushing away the stray ashes. He held the last of a cigarette, tapping it against the edge of the table. "Ah, there we go," he whispered to no one, a smile hovering on his lips as a favoured horse pulled ahead. For a moment, just a moment, hope filled his gaze. "Whatcha at there?" he says to me, puzzled by my young presence in the place.

I held my Yorkie bar tight, fingers almost making it melt. The package said Not for Girls, which made me cling to it even more. Da had his eyes glued to the screens, tracking the jockeys and their horses moving toward the start gate.

"Scudamore is looking like a hot favourite, c'mmonnnn Cill Dare me darlin!" the man shouted, nearly swallowing his fag in excitement. It was plain my answer wasn't needed.

I caught it early, the buzz of gambling in our parts, much like Mass but with poorer odds. Mondays were drearier than a wet cat, scraping by with pockets emptier than the local TD's promises. But Fridays, Fridays were magic. Da's social money hit, and suddenly there was life in our pockets, a few coins making music.

Inside the bookies, the air full of ciggie smoke, the papers rustled, voices calling out odds. Grown fellas with Sun newspapers squeezed tight under armpits, pens perched on ears. The Sun's Racing Post rustled, the jingle of loose change in trouser pockets, the sharp snap of paper as bets were torn from pads, feet shuffling on the dirty, worn carpet. The carpet spoke of spilled drinks and lost wages, but behind the ashtrays and mutterings, hope lived there, minute by minute, race by race. I perched on a red stool, watching Da as he eyeballed the racing lists pinned to the wall. Da tossed aside the fag and popped a Fisherman's Friend into his mouth.

"Want one?" He held out the sweets.

I scrunched my nose. "They'll burn the head off of me!"

"Ah, you'll be grand. Are ya alright?" he asked, patting my head. "We'll get a nice treat in Buckley's on our way out from Mullingar."

Swearing came from every angle. "Will ya keep it down lads!" and shushes filled the room. Then, a loud shout burst through, "That's a sure thing at Cheltenham!"

"Galway races! Who's for Galway?" A girl's voice, sharp as a whistle, sliced through all the quiet talk. She was one of the two girls who worked at the bookies, the one with the face that made you stop and stare. Her cheeks had these perfect dimples that seemed to smile even when she didn't. Her blonde hair like gold, so smooth it looked like she'd borrowed it from a fairy Cinderella. The men would lean over the counter, their voices all wobbly, saying things like, "So beautiful, I'd put all my bets on you."

She'd flash a grin and flirt back, "You're definitely a winner today, sweet cheeks," and they'd go red as tomatoes. She knew exactly how to play the lads; they were like little puppies to her.

Another bookie girl shouted, "And we've got the best from Punchestown! Who's feeling lucky?" The other girl wasn't as pretty, but there was something about her. She seemed kinder. On some Fridays, while Miss Pretty chatted with the lads, she'd help the cleaning lady tidy up the place. I watched her as she worked; she had this gentle way with people, an energy that felt warm and welcoming, though I couldn't quite put words to it. Her hair was always in a bun, and she had freckles just like mine.

Da ruffled my hair, a quick, rough pat. "You ok?"

"Grand," I said. "Eh, Da, are ya putting a few bets today or just the one?" I asked, barely reaching his elbow.

He waved me off, his gaze never leaving the screen. "In a minute, this one's a sure thing," he says.

"They're always a sure thing Da," I said. I was bored of swirling around on the red stool.

Laughter burst from behind us, where a group of lads had been listening in. "Ah Jim, looks like your young one's got more sense than ye!" one of them chuckled.

Da joined in the laughter, but right before he could come up with a smart reply, there she was, the bookie girl: "And they're off at Leopardstown!"

she called out, slicing through the noise. The room fell quiet as though someone hit pause on a record player. Everyone turned to watch. As for me, I was wondering if Leopardstown was full of real leopards, running about, giving the horses a good chase.

Da muttered something low. A prayer, or a curse, it was hard to tell.

And then, as quick as it started, the race was over. Da's horse, Speedy Sean, was more of a Slowpoke Sean. "Sure, a snail would have been quicker," he muttered, flinging his paper into the wire bin.

There I was, perched like a bird on the stool, legs dangling, not quite touching the ground. To my right stood Old Mickey, a man so thin you'd lose him if he turned sideways, clinging to his betting slip with fingers like iron twigs, his knuckles white. His eyes, two shining orbs, nearly popped out of his head with every twist and leap of the horses on the telly. "C'mon, ya beauty," he'd whisper, as if he could will the horse faster with his quiet prayer.

Then, across the way, there was Big Joe. He was as large as a bear with a temper to match, especially when luck didn't go his way. Every now and then, he'd let out a groan from the soul of him, so mournful it would make the saints weep. "Ah, Jaysus, not again," he moaned.

The twins, Mary and Martha, were peas in a pod but as different as chalk and cheese when it came to the races. Mary, with her notebook full of numbers and odds, scribbled away like she was cracking some code. Martha, on the other hand, picked her horses the same way she'd pick lads at the Greville Arms on a Saturday night. If they had a nice name or a shiny coat, they were the one for her. "Ooh, I like the sound of Galloping Gerty," she laughed, oblivious to Mary's eye-rolling.

Just then the bookies received a surprising visitor. Tommy Dowd walked in. Everyone knew him. He was middle-aged but looked ancient, like those old tree roots in the Derrygreenagh Forest, tough and twisted from all the 'not so nice' things he'd done. He was the most successful businessman in Mullingar, but the sources of his success were shadowy and unclear. Da said Tommy left school early to work on the farm, then worked at the Bord before figuring out all about business on his own. "Big brain, that one," Da would say, "Dangerous to be that smart."

He had bright blue eyes and a shock of wild hair streaked with chestnut and grey, looking like he'd just got out of bed. Across his left cheek was a deep scar from the car crash in 1989. He'd been the driver that day when his wife was killed and since then a black cloud hovered over him everywhere, settling into a permanent scowl that made him fearsome to look at. Tommy went straight to the counter and placed a few bets with Miss Pretty. He was frowning but that was nothing new. Tommy's missus was dead and he wasn't letting any of us forget it.

In my little corner, I continued to swirl on my stool, a silent watcher. Every race was a story, every shout and sigh a tale of triumph or disaster. Oh, we'd laugh, especially when Seamus, who fancied himself a bit of a poet, tried to rhyme his way into fortune. "If Galloping Gerty hits the post, I swear I'll turn her into roast," Seamus declared, only for the room to erupt into giggles as Gerty galloped home, leaving Seamus to munch on his words instead of his winnings. Tommy remained silent as a post, not the beginnings of a smile on him. And there was Da on the edge of his seat, his eyes glued to the screen again. Every click of that pretty girl's keyboard was like a drumroll, building up to some grand event that could end in either cheers or tears.

I shifted on my stool, the vinyl sticking to my legs. Suddenly, the room held its breath as the latest race came to its frantic end. Da's face twisted in a mixture of hope and dread; his horse was coming up fast, closing the distance inch by inch.

"Come on, come on!" Da's voice, usually a low, gravelly mumble, rose to a fever pitch.

As the horses barrelled towards the finish line, the room erupted into shouts and groans. Da's horse, an underdog named Whispering Wind, crossed the line first by a nose.

An explosion of relieved laughter and high-fives broke out around us. Da leaped up, a rare, broad grin splitting his face. He wasn't a rich man, but he had that look in his eyes, that glimmer of victory that made it all worthwhile. "Jaysus, I've done it again! Yahoooooooo!" He shouted, running about the room like the happiest man on earth.

"Heh, Da," I whispered, "You're causing a scene, jeez."

"A scene, is it?" He laughed, breaking into a little jig. "This isn't a scene, it's going to be a great week, no trips to Bradley's this week, that's what it is."

Nancy Mooney burst in through the doors, her little baby lamb, Millie Moo, trotting right beside her. "I won! I won at Leopardstown!" she shouted, making sure everyone heard. She shot up to the counter, demanding her winnings. "It was ten to one, and I laid a tenner on him!" she boasted, as if the bookies instantly knew every person's bet off pat. She wore an oversized navy flowery dress and welly boots with what looked like a tea cosy perched on her head. Her pink lipstick was smudged to the right of her mouth, and a brooch of the Irish flag dangled from her sizeable right bosom.

"Show us your ticket, love," said Miss Pretty.

"Ticket, ticket..." Nancy mumbled, patting her pockets. With a theatrical swivel she turned around and crouched down, scanning the floor. A groan of despair welled up within her. Then defiance took over. She straightened up and turned back to face her accuser. "I definitely won—let God be my witness! My horse, Living Next Door to Alive, came in at ten-to-one at Leopardstown!"

Miss Pretty sighed, smoothing out the slips. "Without your betting slip I can't help you my love."

A toothless man in the corner chortled, "Sure, isn't that Peep's lamb?" Laughter echoed, and voices burst from every direction.

Nancy's face crumpled, tears welling up. She looked down at Millie Moo and whispered, "Is no one going to believe me?" The silence was her answer and at that moment Nancy let out a roar, an animal outpouring of despair.

"Ahh sorry Nancy," the kinder bookie lady looked at her with sympathetic eyes. "Maybe next time, Nancy."

The crowd decided the scene had gone on long enough. “Go on, Nancy, get off with ye,” they jeered.

Broken, Nancy began to leave the bookies, wiping away her tears. “To hell with the lot of you,” she blurted out.

Da and I remained silent, onlookers to this public downfall. My heart broke for Nancy, but I knew the risks. She could turn on you, and she had done so before. Of all people, Tommy stepped forward, his eyes scanning Nancy with curiosity. “Nancy, I tell you something. Can you look me in the eye and tell the truth? Did you put a tenner down? Swear on Millie Moo’s life that you did?”

Nancy’s face twisted with doubt. A flash of the earlier Nancy came back to her. “I did, I swear I did!” she bellowed.

Tommy paused, leaning closer, “And when did you place the bet?”

Her words stumbled over each other: “This morning, I did. Oh wait—yesterday, I mean an hour ago...” The crowd in the bookies watched the drama. My heart felt like it was carrying a boulder for her. I glanced at Da’s face and saw the same weight in his eyes.

“An hour ago you say?” Miss Pretty said. “What’s this?” she said, holding the bookie’s notebook for Leopardstown. "Win or lose, young woman, the reality of it is now upon us."

The room fell silent, every eye on Miss Pretty as she opened the notebook and ran her finger down the list of winners. She raised an eyebrow in surprise. "Well, would you look at that, 10 on Living Next Door to Alive to win at 10-to-1. No one's claimed it yet. Too bad you lost the slip, love."

Nancy's sorrow quickly shifted to glee, and she grabbed Millie Moo, spinning her around. Being proved right was compensation for losing the evidence that would have secured her winnings. The crowd erupted. Some cheered, some groaned, and others shook their heads in disbelief. Only Tommy's face softened, amusement turning into something close to sympathy. "Nancy, maybe next time, keep the ticket away from Millie Moo, alright?"

"I will, Tommy! Maybe even buy the lass a nice scarf to chew on!"

Tommy was silent for a moment, and then bent down and patted the lamb. It was the oddest gesture coming from him. There was another pause and then he said quietly, "Alright, Nancy. Tell you what. Here's what I'll do. I'll give you the 100. You lost your ticket, but I believe you even if them lot don't," Tommy said.

The people around us murmured, eyebrows lifting in astonishment. One boy, who thought he was funny, shouted, “Sure, let’s all lose our tickets, then!” His laugh echoed, but Tommy’s glare shut him up faster than a rabbit into a burrow.

Tommy took out the 100 and passed it to Nancy. She hugged him tight, whispering, “Oh, thanks a million, thanks a million. There is a God, oh, there is.” The rest of us just stood there, blinking, wondering how Tommy—sharp as a tack—could be so kind and, maybe, just a little bit silly.

“Should we head home?” Da asked, counting his winnings. “No St Vincent de Paul’s corned beef this week,” he grinned.

As we stepped outside, a betting slip stuck to my shoe. I picked it off and opened it up. 10 at 10/1 on Living Next Door to Alice. Heart thumping, I considered the options. 100 punt! My hand was shaking as I closed my fist over the betting slip. But at that very moment of doubt and temptation, Da spotted me and asked what I was holding. Without a word, I walked up to Tommy and handed it over. He glanced at it, then at me, a smile finally breaking out across his lips.

“Sure, she might be mad, but she’s no liar. You’re a good girl,” Tommy said, pressing a 50 pence into my hand.

Dawn Raid

"We're off to the field."

Da stood by the bedroom door waiting, his duffle coat hung over his shoulders like a magician's cloak.

"Are you getting up?" He pressed his finger to his lips. "Don't wake the rest of them," he added, his gaze holding mine with gentle insistence.

I squirmed out of the cramped bed, wriggling myself free from the nest of sisters. They were my warm cocoon, like hot water bottles on a chilly night. Their limbs were snug and heavy, making it hard to leave the cozy pile. But the day and Da was calling.

When I broke free from the bed the cold hit me like a splash of icy water. Shivers chased down my spine as I climbed into my clothes, the damp fabric sticky against my skin. Little puffs of fog escaped my mouth. For a second, I imagined I was a dragon.

Peering into the kitchen, I saw Da clearing ashes from the range.

"Let's get going," he whispered.

"I'm ready, Da," I said, grabbing my jacket and tugging the hood over my head.

I grabbed two plastic bags from the coal hole and shoved a slice of soda bread into my pocket, just in case. Da had the kettle of hot water in his hand, for the icy Fiat which he poured all over the windscreen and the bonnet. The car steamed and sizzled, startled out of its frozen trance.

Derrygreenagh Park was wreathed in the quiet of early morning, chimneys yawning out thin tufts of smoke. No one else was awake yet, just us, breaking the stillness. "Come on, get in, we need to get on before the sun gets us," Da whispered, conspiratorially.

"Oh Da, I forgot to bless myself," I blurted out. Guilt gripped me. How could I forget? Mrs Bollard brought the holy water all the way from Lourdes. Our little font above the porch table was as blessed as the most blessed holy water font in the neighbourhood.

"Da, can I run back and grab a drop?" I pleaded.

"Go on, hurry up. It'll be lunchtime before we know it."

"Grand, Da, I won't be two minutes!" As I reached into the font with my index and middle finger, I silently intoned, "In the name of the Father, the Son, and the Holy Spirit." I breathed a little easier as I eased the front door shut. It was like I had a top security detail of guardian angels watching over me now. I was now free from the fires of Purgatory.

The car's engine made a retching sound as Da turned the key, and its first hop forward nearly resulted in an icy skid. The road was so empty you'd think it was all ours, saying good morning only to the big lorries that rumbled by, packed with goodies for people I'd never meet, living in places I'd never heard of. And then came the Hill of Uisneach, like a giant's shoulder we had to climb.

I thought about that old story Auntie Veronica loved to tell, how Da was all set to be a priest before he met Mammy. The idea of him in a priest's robes made my stomach do a funny flip. If Da had taken that holy path, would we even be here today, in the car on a frosty morning, two thieves at dawn. Would I be alive?

"Da, do ya really think I have to jump that electric fence?"

Da's laugh bubbled up. "Ah, don't be worrying. We'll slide ya right under it," he said. "While you're gathering them, I'll nip over to Fitzpatrick's, see if I can get us a few bits for the week. That tab at Bradley's couldn't stretch any farther if it tried. I'll be in and out of Fitzpatrick's before the early birds even think of stirring."

I felt a bit of the tension melt away, nodding. Da always had a way of making things seem doable, even the scary bits.

"Da, are ya sure there's no cattle in the field? Or bulls?"

"Ah no. I wouldn't drop you in a field full of beasts. Not on purpose, anyway," he added with a mischievous grin.

We reached our destination. "That's where the O'Sullivans live," Dad nodded toward an imposing farmhouse, built of mass concrete, as big as any home in the county. The farmhouse was set back from the road, reached by a wide gravel drive, and set in a beautifully manicured valley. Beyond that, field upon field of spring barley.

"He doesn't realize how lucky he is," Da says. "Look at all this land he owns. Half of Westmeath stretching in every direction. But all the same he's not happy is auld O'Sullivan. His only boy, aged 11, killed stone dead. By a horse's kick. Wham, right in the head. Everyone has their secret crosses to bear don't they, Polly. When you put it like that, we're the lucky ones aren't we?"

"Yes, we are Da, thanks be to God." I said thinking of Ollie Sullivan's son. Thinking sure he was almost the same age as me.

The morning sun painted the farmhouse an off-white, standing out bright against the endless green fields. Compared to O'Sullivan's farmhouse, our two-bed Derrygreenagh home felt tiny, like it could vanish if you blinked too long. I figured you could fit ten of our houses inside it, and they only being two of them and all, not like our 11.

We passed by the farmhouse on our left and chugged to a stop on a side road, our secret hideout.

"Now, see that gate?" Da whispered, like even the grass might hear. "I'll lift it, you jump under. Grab those blue plastic bags."

"Will ya be long, Da?" My voice was barely there, my heart pounding like mad in my chest.

"No, 30 minutes or so," he assured me. But to me, 30 minutes felt like forever.

"Alright, but hurry, Da. Don't leave me hanging too long," I urged, as we both quietly slipped out of the car, pressing the doors shut gently.

"Come here, keep your head down," Da whispered, eyes flicking to the farmhouse, watching for any twitch of curtains. "Put the big ones in one bag, the smaller ones in another."

"Got it, but don't be late Da."

The field stretched out like a big, green ocean, quiet and eerie. The frost had melted, leaving its residue which made my runners squish with each step. I felt the wetness soak through my socks, but my stomach did that fluttery thing it does when you're excited and scared all at once. The air smelled fresh, with a hint of damp earth.

Da moved toward the fence in a hunched posture. I followed close, gripping the bags tight, feeling mighty important. I was the best at carrying bags, no doubt, and I was side by side with Da on this secret mission, this dawn raid. The silence was upon us, but even though speech was not permitted, it felt like we were having the deepest conversation.

Finally, we reached the fence. Da found an old twig under the big oak tree.

"Da, you're not really gonna touch that electric fence, are you? It'll zap your arm off!" I warned.

"I'm just having a look," he said. He placed the twig on the fence. In a flash, he leaped straight up as if he'd been struck by lightning.

"Da! Da!" I screamed.

"What? What?" he laughed. "Sssssh! I was kidding. It's not on. Auld O'Sullivan's too cheap to keep it running. Might cost him a bob or two."

Then Da ditched the twig and lifted the wire as high as he could with his left hand. "In you go," he whispered. I crept under, holding my breath, safe once again.

"See ye soon, Da," I whispered, as he retreated towards the Fiat.

"Ya sure the bull's not about?" I said looking around the field.

Da grinned, "Ah, would ya stop. You'll give yerself a fright before you even begin. Won't be long. Stay around those patches; that's where the mushrooms like to make their appearance."

Da's car departed. I stood alone in the green field, feeling like I'd just dropped from the sky, my heart pounding in my chest. The silence was thick, the grass tickling up my legs. I gave myself a good shake, eyes darting to the big house where O'Sullivan lived, like a giant watching over everything.

"Quick," I said to myself, "you got less than an hour. Gotta fill these bags fast."

My breath came out in one quick whoosh, eyes searching for any sign of them white capped friends.

"God, stop this fear, and like ya rid Ireland of snakes with St. Patrick, get rid of them bulls," I mumbled under my breath, my hands already diving into the work.

I bent down on my hands and knees, fingers poking and prodding the grass for mushrooms. One bag snug in my back pocket, the other open, waiting for the pickings.

Even with the chill nipping at my toes, something warmed inside. There was a certain magic to this place. "Don't you dare think of coming out, sun," I muttered, half-jokingly. The sun made it harder to spot the mushrooms glistening under dewdrops. The crows, silhouetted against the lightening sky, kept watch, cawing as if mocking my hunt.

I moved from mushroom patch to patch, gently tugging the fungi from their earthen beds. The delicate ones crumbled easily, while the firm, ripe ones popped out with that lovely crunch, the sound of the earth reluctantly letting go. Each one I placed in my bag felt like a treasure, every little cap promising something exotic.

In the distance, I could just make out the gentle hum of O'Sullivan's tractor coming to life. It was a sound grounding me back to the present, a gentle reminder that this sacred morning time was fleeting and full of risk. My gathering turned more urgent.

Wiping the dampness from my brow with a muddy sleeve, I noticed with pride the bags starting to swell. I took a deep breath and looked around. The morning fog had lifted, revealing more of the landscape, rolling hills, patches of wildflowers, and the hearty hedgerows that framed the field.

"Almost done," I whispered to the landscape, as I extracted a particularly plump mushroom nestled against a knotted root. It came free with a satisfying snap, its pale cap glowing in the emerging daylight.

Bag filled, I stood tall, stretching my aching limbs. The crows flew off in a flutter. I cast one last glance around. With a contented sigh, I turned back towards the distant frame of the farmer's house. My bags were so stuffed, I could barely carry them. And as for Da's sorting rules? Forget it! Big ones, tiny ones, all mixed up in one big mixture. I took a peek inside one of the bags. The mushrooms were a sight to look at! Some were like grand lords with fancy hats, others like shy maids in simple bonnets, and a few were skinny as beanpoles. And the colours! Some were pale as ghosts, others brown as old boots, and a couple even managed to look grumpy.

Every squishy step I took in my soggy shoes felt like the field was whispering secrets to me. Each little mushroom was like a hidden treasure, waiting to be found.

Then as if from nowhere the tractor crested a hill just ahead of me on the field. There was nowhere to go, so I just froze. The tractor was coming right towards me. It stopped short of me and down leapt auld O'Sullivan, the victim of my dawn raid. He was round and kind of jolly, like a big, overstuffed teddy bear. His cheeks were as red as apples, and his eyebrows looked like they could sweep the floor, all bushy and wild. His lips were this funny mix of red and purple, and when he grinned, you could see his pink, baby-like gums and small teeth that made him look like he never grew up properly.

"Well now, what are you up to?" he asked.

"Just picking some mushrooms," I said nervously. "I'm sorry," my voice trailed off, no match for his booming vocal.

"Well, is that a thing. You do know you're on my land, young lady," Mr O'Sullivan observed, his face serious.

"Oh, I was just... borrowing these," I stammered, looking down at the blue bags filled with mushrooms.

Mr O'Sullivan stood just a few yards away. He took some steps closer, his eyes scanning the bags at my feet. "Those are my mushrooms, you know. You're on my land, my land and my field. The field of my family and my father's father."

"I'm sorry, Mr O'Sullivan," I stammered. "I didn't mean any harm. We don't do it often and the field is full of them. And, and... we didn't want to wake anyone, otherwise we would've asked."

"I know what it's like to need, you have no idea, girl." There was a long pause, the only sound the gentle rustling of the wind through the grass. Then, Mr O'Sullivan spoke again, his voice quieter. "How many brothers and sisters do you have?"

"There's nine of us, five girls and four boys," I said, lifting my eyes to meet his. "All crammed together like sardines in 56 Derrygreenagh Park. It's a madhouse. I'm number six and even if I'm almost in the middle I'm the least quiet!"

He nodded slowly. "Must be nice, having a big family."

"It is," I said. "But it can be hard sometimes, especially sharing the bed half the time with my sisters. I send Tracey up some nights to be the hot water bottle; she warms it up first, then we all jump in. I think she makes Caroline and Aine do it too. We all take turns, but they're annoying sometimes. And the brothers can be nice, but we pull the heads off each other too."

Mr O'Sullivan's eyes softened.

"Well, I suppose a few mushrooms won't hurt. But you must promise me something."

"Anything, Mr O'Sullivan."

He smiled. "You're a very lucky girl," he said.

"And you too, look at your big house and so many fields and you must be very rich," I said.

Mr O'Sullivan sniffed, rubbing his reddened nose. He made as if to say something but stopped.

We both just stood there for a few moments, each with our thoughts.

Mr O'Sullivan nodded, as if he could hear my thoughts. "Hold on to that, young Heavey," he said softly. "You're a lucky girl."

"I promise," I said.

He reached down and picked up one of the bags, handing it to me. "Go on, take these. And tell your Da he's welcome to come by any time, as long as he asks first."

"Thank you, Mr O'Sullivan."

As I turned to leave, I glanced back at him one last time. He was standing there, looking out over the field. Then with a quick wave he climbed into the cockpit of his tractor. The sun was clear of the dawn haze, spreading more and more warmth as it climbed into view.

A Derrygreenagh Girl

Dear Lord, hear my prayer. I live in Derrygreenagh Park with Ma, the four brothers, the four sisters and Bingo Heavey. I am 14. I am a good girl. At least I try to be. I've shared my Fat Frogs, Snow Balls, Stinger Bars, Mr Freezers and Refreshers with the younger ones. I've carried the bales of briquettes, the bags from Bradley's and the tinned corned beef from St Vincent de Paul's. I hardly swore, never stole, at least not from strangers, and not counting that roll of twenties out of Da's suitcase from the redundancy money which I invested wisely with the bingo books and the horses and tried to double my money by topping up on All Cash tickets to win the jackpot.

In the name of the Father, and of the Son, and of the Holy Spirit.

So all things considered I have been more often good than not, well apart from playing Ouija with the Scrabble board with all the pieces and taking off our confirmation chains and the nuns finding out about it and thinking we were black magic devil worshippers. Listen God, I am sorry, please forgive me but why oh why did you have you take him away from me? Him of all people? And on Father's Day of all days?

Glorious St. Patrick, you are honoured as one of the greatest evangelists, and true defenders of our faith, that enabled you to bring the light of the true faith to all of Ireland. Intercede for me and place my special intentions before Christ.

I promise, I'll do better this time. I'll even go back to the bookies with him without whining. I'll be nicer to Nancy Mooney, even when she's being a pain. No more moaning about the Joy Riders on my way to Bettystown. I won't grumble at the bog, no matter how muddy it gets. And I'll carry all the bags from Bradley's without a single complaint. And Mutt Fennelly? I won't say a bad word about him, I swear.

May my petition receive a favourable response if it be for the greater honour and glory of God and my own soul.

Perhaps you can bring him back, just for one day like, one final farewell and we can take a walk up Tinkers Hill and I can carry the cans of hand-out corned beef and let Da walk in front, one lanky stride to my three, and I can tell him how much I loved him and how truly sorry I am for being naughty.

Bettystown, the Irish Florida

"Grab the Joy Riders, quick!" Ma says. Da pulls out the pills, one by one, passing each of us a cup of water. We're perched on the couch, the five of us, our bums barely fitting on the worn-out cushions. It feels like we're about to take our first Holy Communion.

I pop the Joy Rider into my mouth, it fizzes pleasantly, fruity and fizzy on my tongue before I wash it down with a swill of water.

It was the older brother's turn this time, as he and the sisters stuffed their bags for our half-family day out. Caroline shot out a question that we were all thinking, "Is she coming soon or what? I don't have all day to be waiting."

Da raised an eyebrow and replied, "Sit down, you. If you don't take that Joy Rider you're going nowhere. You'll be stuck with me, peeling spuds for the older ones."

"No, I won't!" Caroline yelled and grabbed Baby Dumps' hand, shouting, "We're off to Bettystown, we're off to Bettystown!" Their little dresses twirled and swirled as they spun around until they got all dizzy.

"Oh, she's here!" Tracey shouts. We all snapped up straight as rods, ears pricking at the sound of the car door clacking open.

"Hello, hello, anyone at home?" Auntie Pauline's voice floated in.

"Come in, come in, Pauline," Da said from the doorway.

And there was Auntie Pauline. She had on a habit and a sky-blue blouse. A light grey skirt breezed around her legs. It wasn't disco clothes but you could feel she was ready for an adventure. This was different. This was Pauline, not Sister Labore or Sister Pauline, or even Auntie Pauline, but just Pauline. She grabbed a stack of newspapers by the door.

"When a child's bum is on newsprint, they never get sick," she said. She must've been joking with the younger ones, but I played along. I could see the younger ones frowning thinking: *were the newspapers laid out to keep the car clean from puke, or did they have some kind of magic powers? I mean Auntie Pauline was a nun, after all. She wouldn't lie, God was always listening.* I always admired Auntie Pauline. I wanted to be just like her until I turned seven. I thought all nuns drove around in cars, gave food to the poor and lived with their best friends in a dormitory. But then I heard Da telling Ma one night that all the nuns of the convent had to share just one car.

"Come on children, let's get a move on!" Auntie Pauline said holding a stack of newspapers under her arm. Without a second's pause, we became a wild stampede, racing each other to the car. We were geared to conquer the world, newspapered and Joy Ridered, ready to brave the road to Bettystown without a single puke pitstop. Auntie Pauline spread out the newspapers, and we hurled our plastic bags into the backseat.

"Move over! Get off me! I'm at the window," Caroline says.

"No, I am," Tracey shot back.

"No, me," Baby Dumps jumped in.

"You can all have a go later," Auntie Pauline said. Liam jumped into the front, claiming his spot without any fuss. Ma and Da stood on the front doorstep, waving us off. Auntie Pauline gripped the steering wheel as we left Derrygreenagh and turned right onto the main Mullingar road. No thumbing stop for me this time, and no getting soaked either. We were on a road trip to Bettystown.

"Shall we say the Motorist's Prayer boys and girls?" she glanced at us in the rearview mirror, beckoning us to raise our chins. "Before we take our place," she began then paused, as we repeated after her, "Behind this wheel we pray, oh Sacred Heart of

Jesus guide us on our way. Virgin Mary, morning star, from every danger guard this car. Thou Dear Lord who gave it to enjoy, grant its purpose be to save and not destroy."

"Amen," we chorused.

Squished like sardines, bouncing together in the back seat, me and the three sisters began singing, *We've Got the Whole World in Our Hand*s at the top of our lungs. Auntie Pauline looked ahead of her as Liam kept watch for potholes, and it felt like we were a choir of nuns or something, with all of us perfectly out of tune.

"Hold onto your hats, girls! We're off to Bettystown!" Auntie Pauline said in her sing song way. In my head version, she was screaming "Yeehaw!" like a cowgirl at a rodeo. The car rocked and rolled, and I couldn't stop giggling. I felt as though I was an explorer heading out on a wild adventure.

"Keep the singing going, this is our adventure!" Auntie Pauline called out, her voice full of excitement. We kept up with our singing but messed with the words. "We got Tracey and Thomas in our hands, we got Tracey and Tommy in our hands," we sang, giggling as we swapped the lyrics to tease our sisters about their school crushes that year.

Tracey's cheeks flushed bright red. "I don't even like Thomas," Tracey huffed. "It's more like Caroline and Thomas. I caught them in Cully's arch kissing," she blurted out.

"No, you didn't!" Caroline looked imploringly at Auntie Pauline, especially since she'd mentioned kissing right in front of a nun. "You're dead meat when we get home," says Caroline giving Tracey a dirty look.

Beside me, Tracey held onto her map of Meath pointing at Laytown like it was full of secret treasure. Laytown was just down the coast from Bettystown. We were all pretending we knew how to read the map, but none of us had a clue.

"Can you see what road we're on, Liam?" asked Auntie Pauline. We had a funny feeling we were a little lost on the old bog roads.

"I will, Auntie Pauline," said Liam. "Hand it over to me, girls. Let the real brains do it." Tracey reluctantly passed over the map while we stuck our fingers up at the older brother without letting Auntie Pauline see. I mean, she was a nun and all.

Down by our squished-up feet, Caroline, with her blonde pigtails, was lost in thoughts of the teacups ride. "We're still going to the amusements, right?" she asked.

"Well, that's if we ever get there," I whispered in her ear.

"Of course we are going to the amusement park," she shouted, as I tried to shush her.

And then there was Baby Dumps clutching her blankey tight, her tiny fingers wrapped around a shiny twenty pence Da had given her. She whispered to me, "I'm gonna scream so loud." Her wide eyes looked at me in wonderment, as if not quite believing she too was part of this adventure.

"Can we get those long pink rocks like we did last year, Auntie Pauline?" Caroline asked, nearly licking an invisible rock. She clung to the punt she'd earned from the neighbours, having told everyone in Derrygreenagh about her exciting day holiday. The car drove happily along with our excited chat. Each bump and rumble from the road beneath us felt like we were already in the amusement park. Auntie Pauline consulted with Liam and the map, steering the Opel ever closer to Bettystown. Sure in our heads Bettystown had expanded until it reached the sky itself, a Disneyland of castles and roller coasters and screaming, happy families.

I peered at Caroline; her cheeks were as pale as a ghost, all the colour washed away. Poor thing clung to her little polka-dot dress like a lifeline, her face all scrunched up. "Just think; you'll be on that Florida beach soon, you wouldn't be wanting that pink rock so," I said.

Ever watchful, Auntie Pauline turned her head. A knowing look in her eyes, she called out, "Will I let that window down?"

The wind whipped her words away as she reached back with a blue plastic bag, as if offering a flag of surrender to the relentless road. Caroline snatched the bag with a shaky mitt and began her violent roar with the bag in the backseat.

"Are you alright, Caroline," I whispered, feeling my own stomach doing cartwheels, fighting to stay where it ought to be as I patted her hair and offered her a tissue. Tracey had other thoughts on her chest. "Why didn't the Joy Riders work, and the newspapers?"

We could see drops of sweat on Caroline's brow, and her face seemed to relax a bit in the breeze from Auntie Pauline's open window.

"I'll be fine," she said, though her voice wavered a bit. "I might be a bit hungry." Sure when was she ever not, I thought to myself.

"You can be in the front on the way back," Liam offered with a great show of generosity, as he wound down his window. "Aye but the smell of ya!"

We all burst into laughter, even Caroline, who managed a small smile through her discomfort. Little Aine, still grinning from ear to ear, added in her small voice, "Can I have Caroline's spot if she doesn't want it?"

Tracey chuckled, "We'll see about that, Aine. Maybe by the end of the day, we'll let you swap places!"

With the windows down, fresh air whirled through the car. The road ahead didn't feel so tough any more, and the beach seemed more exciting than ever. Even Caroline's faint smiles felt like little victories.

Aunt Pauline's car glided into the car park at Bettystown, and the smell of the sea was upon us. "Guess where we are, girls!" Pauline shouted, glancing back at us through the front mirror.

"Bettystown!" we all yelled together our voices bursting with excitement.

We'd finally arrived at our Irish Florida, the place we'd been dreaming about all year long. All those nights in the bed tent, whispering and giggling about this day, and now it was here! Just us sisters, Liam, and Pauline at our final stop. Bettystown!

There it was, more rugged and wild than our dreams, an Irish painting of deep greens, greys, and browns, not the golden sands and blue waves we'd imagined. Gravel crunched under the tyres as we glided to a halt alongside other families, popping up boots full to bursting with baskets and plastic coolers, the call of the Irish ocean undeniable.

We spilled out, our feet splashing into car park puddles, tiny ripples mirroring our eager faces.

Used to Westmeath lakes, this was a different beast, the wild Irish Sea. Caroline jumped out first, her red ribbons fluttering among her blonde curls.

"Jaysus, it's fairly windy here!" Liam's voice struggled against the gale. The beach lay before us, not the golden sands of Florida, but something pebbly, both real and roaring.

Our first sight of the sea left us breathless. Before we even touched the pebbly sand, Caroline dashed off, squealing, "It's like pirate land!"

Aine wasn't far behind, yelling, "Finders keepers losers weepers!"

The sea was like a craggy old neighbour, nothing like the shiny postcards of Florida. Sure, those postcards show golden beaches and sunshine, but Bettystown? It gave us pebbles and seashells and seaweed. Catching a glimpse of sand between it all was like finding treasure. Kids ran around, noses purple from the cold, but they didn't care, and their ice creams remained stubbornly solid.

"Girls, get them shoes off ye!" Auntie Pauline's voice rang out, cutting through the roaring air. "Let the ocean tickle your toes, but Lord save us, no splashing about in the waves. Sure, the sea would wipe you out."

Balancing on one foot at a time, we peeled off our runners and socks. It was a long time since our feet had felt sand. They sank into the dark, cold grey between the pebbles and the rocks. We took turns passing Baby Dumps' hand among us, each feeling the small fingers wrap around our own as we danced to the shore's edge.

"Hey, quick dip, dare ya!" I challenged Tracey, a smile spreading across my face.

"And turn into a Mr. Freezer? No thanks."

We marched on, a merry band of sisters and Liam setting our sights on the teacups and the dizzy heights of the Ferris wheel.

"We'll have some food after your rides," Aunt Pauline said, her voice carrying the promise of tin foil treasures, hard-boiled eggs, brown bread, coleslaw, and beetroot, Tracey's favourite.

We'd reached the amusement park. "Holy jeez, will ye look at the Ferris wheel, it could do with a drop of oil... or ten!" Liam says pointing at the creaking giant, groaning louder than an old man with a bad back.

Caroline was having none of it. "It's like Disneyworld!" she clapped her hands, embracing the rust as if it were part of the magic. Tugging on Auntie Pauline's coat, Baby Dumps shrieked, "Can we, can we? I wanna go on the teacups!" she begged, hopping on my toes.

"Of course dear. Now remember girls, hold on tight!" shouted Auntie Pauline, when we launched off on the teacups; but we weren't listening, the older ones with their hands already in the air waving back at her.

Later, we took refuge behind a windbreaker. "C'mere, give us a hand with the stuff from the boot. Look, the wind's easing up and the sky's behaving!" Auntie Pauline says. A rickety wooden bench turned into a banquet table, and in that moment, I was given a royal duty. Pauline handed me the prized possession – a red and white checkered tablecloth.

"Will ye get some rocks?" I ordered the sisters, as I spread it out. They ran down the beach, and brought back the stones, pressing them down on our cloth like it was a wild dog escaping. Liam and Auntie Pauline lugged the mighty basket of grub to our pebbly throne. Above, seagulls circled and hollered, as Pauline shooed them away almost angrily. She was determined to have this feast whatever nature may throw at us. Pauline set out paper plates and we dug into our picnic, chatting about our rides. Who screamed loudest? Who was the bravest? And who spun till they almost hurled?

"Auntie Pauline, are them clouds turning grey?" Liam asked, his eyes squinting at the moody sky.

"Ah, don't mind them, they're only pretending," Pauline replied. But just as we settled in, raindrops began to tap-dance on our spread, and the wind picked up.

"One photo before the rain really starts," Pauline said, pulling out her Polaroid. We squeezed together on one side of the beach, me, the three sisters, and Liam all munching on cucumber and egg sandwiches. In the background, a seagull swooped low, eyeing the food that seemed about to fly in all directions thanks to the wild wind. A white plastic bag of shells rested on the table, its contents peeking out, and our jackets and hair whipped around in the gale. Our smiles beamed, happiness determined to shine through. As cold and pebbly as the deep Irish Sea itself, this was our Irish Florida.

The Shadow

I'd heard Nancy Denehen say that if you believe and put all your trust in the Novena, your wish will come true. I finished the Novena, time passed, and I forgot about it. Then one sunny day, I was lying on the mattress beside Ma and Da's bed.

The mattress was so low that I could peek under the bed, revealing all sorts of things the siblings had hidden from each other: Caroline's Barbie dolls dressed in plastic-bag clothes, Tracey's fancy paper box, and an old diary with a horse cover and a big lock, almost as big as the lock hanging from my own press above the bed. I spotted Da's Sacred Heart picture, the one he always carried in his back pocket with his black comb.

There I was, probably on my 100th reading of one of my artist magazines. This one was about Van Gogh and *Starry Night*. With the room's lightbulb blown, the only light came from the landing. Lying on the dangerous, spring-popping mattress, I suddenly turned to my right and saw a long shadow lift from the bed. It gently moved up, as if dancing.

I didn't realise it then, but that shadow was the greatest thing to enter my young life, my world changed after it appeared.

As soon as the shadow rose, in my mind it was about to turn and look at me. I shot out of that room. At first, I thought my mind was playing tricks, but the clear outline of the figure left no space for doubt in my mind. In those precious moments, despite my fear, I knew that all the beauty and meaning of my 14 short years was contained in a shadow in Mammy and Daddy's bedroom at No. 56. And wherever there is a shadow, there is always light.

Mulvin's Bog

We set out on the seven-mile journey from No. 56 to Knockdrin at 7.30 in the morning. The sun had barely risen, the sky fading from dawn charcoal into morning grey. The chilly air and the dripping dew encouraged us to move smartly.

This time he let me tag along, the older brother. I was twelve, an extra pair of hands and a puffed-out chest. I was proud to be asked to work the bog, especially with Liam. I'd come to the bog with Da and Liam before, mostly to keep me busy, but this was different. This time, coins jingled in the promise. I lay awake thinking about it all.

We each had two plastic bags wrapped around our hands. These bags contained our sandwiches of luncheon meat and salad cream between soft, white slices of Brennan's bread from Joe Delaney's shop. A few custard creams and red lemonade completed our feast.

"You're a great one for coming to the bog," Liam said.

"Ah, sure, I don't mind at all." I was trying to play it cool, but the praise was electric.

"It'll be long days and it will break your back, but you'll meet the lads, and you'll earn a good bit off the Mulvin lad, so don't worry about that."

I was so excited to join Liam on this mission to Mulvin's bog. And at the same time to feel a part of something, an actual job with money changing hands.

We headed off up the Derrygreenagh road, taking a left down the Mullingar road to the village. The roads were quiet, just the occasional voices of me and Liam. "We'll try and thumb a lift," said Liam. We got to the village, past Sluts' Wall, across the road to the sign that pointed to Rhode in Offaly, our destination Knockdrin. The road was full of potholes as we got into our seven-mile trek.

"Will I have a sandwich Liam?" I asked.

"Ah, it's only 7.30, hold out for a bit, the day hasn't even begun." Every time we heard a car behind us, up the thumbs would go, but no cars stopping. On we'd march.

"The turf was cut in May, we have four weeks to get it all footed," Liam explained. He went on to tell me about all the people from the parishes of Moyvalley, Milltown, Ballinabrackey, Edenderry and Ballymore that relied on the turf. About Seamus O'Toole and his stooped back, twisted and bent from years of turf baskets and thinking he was still living in the famine days.

"He can't stand straight ever since," Liam said.

"Poor Bent Seamus," I whispered to myself, nodding my head.

Despite the distance to Mulvin's bog, the journey was not long. A blue Fiat Uno stopped, a man from Offaly eyeing us up like we had something belonging to him.

"Where to, lads?" he enquired, his thick voice lacing each word with a hearty warmth.

"Heading to Knockdrin," Liam replied.

The man chuckled, his eyes crinkling at the corners. "Ah, the boglands! A grand place for getting lost. I'm Seany, Seany Bracken. I knew your father from the Bord," he said. "Jump in! Jump in!" Then in an instant he launched into a story about 'auld Tim Doran'.

We nodded politely to the story of the lost ram of auld Tim Doran, escaping its bounds and getting lost for days in the wild. The image made me want to giggle uncontrollably but I was held in check by the brother listening intently. I didn't want the Offaly man to think I was laughing at him, especially after him stopping for us.

The story continued. "Ah sure there was then five other lads who joined in the search until dusk fell, then wasn't I speaking to Tim the following week and ya won't believe it - Molly the fecking ram was back at the farm that same evening, as if nothing at all had happened. Sure, some cheek. God only knows how it made its way back. Tim says it gladly made its way to his stomach soon enough." He laughed. We nervously laughed with him.

"Oh sure that's mad, Seany, nothing ever surprises me in these parts." Liam said.

The car rumbled along the country roads. The Offaly man turned his attention on to me and said, "Ya see that field over there? Legend has it that the fairies have a grand old time there on moonlit nights, dancing up a storm." Perhaps he imagined I was five, not twelve. Fairies for the love of God. Go away outta that, I thought. "Oh that's nice," I said softly.

We arrived at Mulvin's. As we said farewell, Seany the Offaly man offered one last piece of wisdom. "Mind yourselves with those O'Sullivan twins," he added. "They're as wild as the rams. Good luck."

We jumped out of the car mumbling, "Thanks a million , thanks a million," and waved him off.

"How did he know that the twins were here?" I asked Liam.

"He'd know where ya pissed last, auld Seany the nosey fecker."

"I suppose he gave us a lift all the same, that was decent of him."

The bog stretched out in front of us, endless and wild. A voice floated our way, "Welcome, welcome, young Heaveys!"

"There he goes, Paddy's already at it," Liam said, grinning wide.

Paddy O'Brien came closer, eyes wild like he'd just thought up the greatest trick. He looked straight at me. "You're officially a part of the Bog Workers Club. Give us a bogger handshake," he said.

"What's that?" I asked.

Paddy put out his hand. Just as I reached to shake it, he whipped it back and, with his other hand, handed me a lump of turf. "Let that be your magic lump of turf! Keep it close. It wards off enemies," Paddy said, winking.

"Ah, give it a rest, Paddy," Liam laughed, shaking his head.

I took a moment to look around. I'd often passed the bog in the car to Granny's in Ballinabrackey, but standing on the vast stretch of raw earth was altogether different. The bog was a rich, pigmented realm as dark as a Black Forest Gateau and as textured as tweed, with tints ranging through ochre, olive and emerald to the very brownest of purples. I felt an immediate connection to the earth beneath my feet.

"Our bank's over there," shouted Liam. We had to jump a few bog streams to reach it. Turf banks were measured in perches. One perch was five and a half yards, about five metres. The boundary of our bank was marked with yellow workers' gloves. Yellow stood out as a helpful marker to aid us against the general darkness of the terrain. We reached the bank, but not before jumping the last bog stream. It was wider than I was tall, and it would take a mighty leap to reach the other side. Liam took the great leap and landed on his knees.

"Wow Polly, when you get over this side the view is magic," he said, blue eyes sparkling over at me. He was joined by Paddy. They both looked at me.

"Come on Polly, jump. Take a run at it!"

My heart was in my mouth. If I didn't make it I was going down with the bog bodies – I didn't want to be a sacrifice so young.

"Do it! Do it!" the lads chanted.

I took about ten steps back as a run-up. "Shiittt, ahhh," I screamed as I ran like the clappers. "Aheee!" I launched myself into space, feeling my soul leave my body. Was it my soul or my body which got there first? I grabbed hold of the far side, four hands grabbed mine, then my arms as they pulled me up.

"Welcome, welcome," Paddy exclaimed patting my shoulder. Liam plonked down our bags of sandwiches, red lemonade, and custard creams. The rising sun beamed into my green, excited eyes.

Oliver and Murphy O'Sullivan stood on their bank, their fiery red hair and twinned freckles dancing on their grinning faces. "Hello, lads! Hope you're all fit as fiddles today. We've got a deadly piece of bog to get through," Liam said, eyeing everyone.

"Sure, we were born for this," the twins replied together.

"Who's this girl? A girl at the bog? Shouldn't she be at home doing dishes or cleaning or something?" asked Oliver.

"She's a hard worker," Liam snapped. "She'll give you a run for your money. She's my sister, so keep those words to yourself."

"Jaysus, I was only joking," Oliver replied. To cut through the tension, Oliver piped up in his best Westmeath accent, "Why do sheep go to the movies?"

Murphy rolled his eyes but couldn't help chuckling. "Well, why?"

"They love the baaaaaack row!" Oliver burst into laughter, shoulders shaking as he clutched his sides.

"Be careful of the old bogmen," Oliver said to me. "You know, those Iron Age men that were buried centuries back. They like the blood of young 'uns!"

"Very funny," I replied, but still hoping that I wouldn't come across one.

"These are your lines, Polly," said Liam. He gestured three rows comprised of stacks of 15 pieces of turf, stretching a mile into the distance. The turf had been cut by machine, now us humans had to complete the job by hand. Our mission was to bend over and turn every piece one by one, without gloves. One side was dry, depending on the weather, and it needed to be turned to dry the other side.

"Have a quick sandwich and a drink before you begin," said Liam, "it'll give you energy." I took a swill of red lemonade and a hefty bite of sandwich, salad cream running down my chin. "Don't mind that lad, they're good workers but don't take any heed of them, they have as much intelligence as a slug."

"Yeah, a dead slug!" I added trying to be all cool. With a determination like no other, I met his gaze and declared, "Watch me go!"

Without a moment's pause, I got on with it. One by one, I flipped the sods, arranging them in a perfect row, row after row, until the path stretched as far as the eye could see. I wanted to show him. My hands dug into the earth, the mud cool and sticky between my fingers. Each piece of turf I turned felt like a story waiting to be told. In the distance, bulldozers and peat cutters were busy creating yet more banks of turf. Turning, turning, turning a piece of history, of Medieval history. Maybe I'd discover an ancestor here, an ancient Heavey. Turning, ever turning. I let my mind wander, picturing the ancient bog bodies resting somewhere below. Could one be right under my feet? Preserved perfectly, untouched by time? Mrs Kavanagh's voice, the English teacher, came to me. *I almost love you but would have cast, I know, the stones of silence.* Were these old souls silent in the folds of turf, watching me from beneath?

The lads were always nearby, messing about, tossing stinging nettles and laughing. But here, as I worked, their voices became a distant hum. Being busy with the turf gave me a purpose. My hands and back ached, but I felt an odd sense of satisfaction, a connection to something far greater than myself.

"Ah sure, you must be hungry, children," called Mrs Mulvin.

There she was, padding through the bog, a tray of sandwiches balanced on her hip. Our eyes lit up at the sight. Mrs Mulvin, the mother of 11, small as a robin, with black hair pinned neatly back, always seemed tireless. She could move mountains if she had a mind to. Her house was on the edge of the bog, always bustling with the life of her 11 progeny.

Her tray was a treasure, piled high with ham salad and cheese and salad cream sandwiches. "Here you go now," she said, and we gathered around, grabbing the sandwiches with eager hands. We had our own sandwiches but nothing tasted better than someone's kindness buttered in the middle. "Take a little rest between those lines, the sun's hot enough today so be careful to drink plenty."

Liam said, "We got some red lemonade Mrs Mulvin," holding it up in the air, "but thanks a million."

"I'll be off to feed my own lot," she said after a pause.

I returned to my plot. The sun was burning my back, throwing long shadows all over the big peat bog. My ears got used to hearing the sounds of skylarks whizzing round my head and hares munching on heather and bog cotton. I continued to turn each sod of turf to ensure the sun and wind would help the drying process. Then I placed the turf upright, or *footed*, for further drying. Then I had to place five or six sods of turf upright, leaning against each other. We took breaks every hour or two. The bog dust would find its way even into our sandwiches. Now and again Liam would bring me over a custard cream and I'd wash it down with red lemonade, a combination of sugary delight in the bog fields.

Just then from nowhere, a little frog popped up. A cute little thing, Jesus he jumped right up into my face, leaving a slimy trace. Long hind legs, small fat body, webbed digits, no tail, protruding eyes. Those froggy eyes stared into my green eyes. "Ribbett, ribbett," he said, sharing a furtive glance before, as quick as he had come, he was away. Perhaps he'd passed me a message from my Iron Age ancestors?

"Liam, frogs here," I screamed, but I wasn't the only one with guests.

The O'Sullivan twins had a bucket full of froggies on their muddy bank. Oliver piped up, "Heh, let's turn all the frogs inside out!" Murphy laughed, ready to join in and holding one up in the sunlight.

"What, no!" I screamed. But Liam and Paddy weren't having it. They charged at the twins and wrestled them to the ground. The frogs took their chance, hopping away in a green blur. The twins ended up face down in the muck.

"If ye do that again, ye can feck off the bog. I'll get two other lads," Liam warned.

The twins scrambled up, brushing themselves off, not saying a word. Mulvin paid well, and they had punts on their minds. They quietly got back to work.

"Are ye okay?" I asked, seeing Liam's left hand was bleeding.

"I'm grand," Liam said, trying to smile through the pain. "Won't be a bother on me."

"Jesus, Liam, you need at least a tissue or something. Maybe a plaster. Skinner McCabe's caravan is over there. Not far. I'll run over."

My knuckles barely brushed the dusty caravan door when I whispered, "Mr McCabe? Are ya in?"

From inside, I heard the caravan groan as someone moved. Soon, the door creaked open. There stood Mick (Skinner) McCabe, his blue eyes sharp as ice. "Och, what's happened, girlie? Alana mo cridhe, what's going on? Come in, Sit down."

He had a smile that sort of pulled you in, all soft and nice. He didn't have a lot of hair, just a few tufts here and there on his head. His old green sweater looked like it could tell stories, and his black work pants were worn out. His face was soft and buttery, and his smile showed just a few teeth left, but it was the best grin ever. He had this little hat he kept fixing on his head, and he'd scratch his head sometimes.

"Liam's hand, it's bleeding pretty bad," I blurted out, the words stumbling over each other.

"Is it gonna fall off?" he asked a grin on his eye. How did he know who Liam was?

"Oh, I hope not," I replied, "but there's a lot of blood."

"I'll grab a few things for ya, girlie." He rummaged around, emerging with a clean cloth and a tin of plasters, then nudged me toward the door.

Inside the caravan, holy pictures of God hung on the walls, alongside black and white photos from a time gone by. A little green range sat in the corner, surrounded by neat piles of newspapers and books. Although the furnishings were limited and basic, Skinner kept his caravan in perfect order. "I'll toss in a few bars of Cadbury's and a few bags of crisps for ye," he said, stuffing the goodies into a brown paper bag. "Let's go fix that hand."

"Thanks, Skinner I mean, Mick," I said, embarrassed.

"You can call me Skinner, girlie," he chuckled. "I have many names - bog man, the ghost of Knockdrin, you name it. Skinner's the least of them." He walked straight over to Liam, without me even telling him who he was. "Good lad," Skinner said, "have a few of them," as he handed him the cloth and plasters.

"Alright, young ones, gather round," Skinner announced. "You know, the bog's got its own stories, waiting to be told."

"What kind of stories?" asked a twin.

"The kind that'd make your hair stand on end," Skinner replied, his voice lowering as if sharing a secret. "You ever hear of the Banshee? We were cutting turf one misty morning, and just as the sun rose, a piercing wail echoed across the bog. We froze, too afraid to move. Next day, old Tom Murphy passed away."

The twins gasped, their eyes like saucers.

"Course, there's good stories too," Skinner added quickly. "You treat the bog well, and it'll treat you right back. Around 1935, a fellow found a golden torc buried deep in the turf. Made him richer than he ever dreamed. The bog keeps its secrets, and it keeps its balance. Now, who wants a bar of Cadbury's?"

As the evening wore on, the sky turned a deep indigo.

"Thanks, Mick. For everything," Liam said, his voice soft but sincere.

"Ach, don't mention it," Skinner replied, giving him a warm smile. "Just remember what I said. The bog's got ears, and it's always listening."

With that, Skinner turned and started walking back to his little caravan. His voice rose up in a familiar tune, *The Valley of Knockanure*. I could hear the melody drifting through the air, and it felt like the whole world stopped to listen.

Now the summer sun was setting now
Between the hills and the sea
And the pale pale moon was rising

Far out from Tralee town
And the dismal stars and the clouds afar
Are darkening o'er the moor
And the banshee cried as our sons they died
In the Valley of Knockanure

"Are ya ready to go?" Liam asked as he handed me my two squished-up salad cream sandwiches. "Well done, you got through that."

We started on the return journey just as the summer sun was setting. I was as dirty as the bog, dust and freckles in equal abundance, with bog cotton floating around us. It reminded me of Daddy's soft grey hair.

The Last Walk

"Wait for me, wait for me!" I yelled, my heart beating a million miles an hour at the thought he'd head out that door without me. My father stood framed by the doorway entrance, with the mirror catching the silver and grey in his hair as he ran his little black comb through it, a ritual as regular as the ticking of Our Lady's hallway clock. The comb, snug in the back pocket of his navy trousers, was always on call.

As I ran downstairs I tried to jam my feet into my runners handed down by the cousins from England. I was a size five and a half, these shoes were a four. It didn't matter.

But Da hadn't left yet, half blocking the door, one boot propped up like he was barricading it against an army, the other trying to calm down Bingo Heavey who was having none of it. Bingo was all over the place, yapping, tail wagging like a flag in high winds. Outside, the boys from the estate were shouting at one another, that easy sneering of theirs slicing through the air.

"Gwan, get some holy water on ya," Da says, chucking a few drops my way.

"Ah stop," I said, dodging him, "you're after drowning me."

"In the name of the Father, Son and Holy Ghost," we both murmured like it was a secret between us, God, and the front door.

From the hallway, Mammy's voice comes through, "Go safe on those roads. Don't be there until you're back!"

"Where are we off to, Da?" I asked when the door clicked shut.

"Going to see Granny," he says, dead casual, like we're just popping next door and not traipsing halfway across the country. It was a fair trek to Ballinabrackey, and our Fiat Uno was as dry as a bone. It was a Monday, and we never had any petrol money on a Monday.

"Will we be thumbing it?" I asked, half excited, half dreading the answer.

"Course we will, we'll get there," Da says with a nod popping a Fisherman's Friend into his gob. We set off, Da leading the charge as usual. I started to fall behind, he tossed over his shoulder a "Come on!"

We took a left out of the house, passing 57, 58, and 59, heading to the main Bridge Road. The place was alive, the sounds of the lads kicking a football about, kids zipping back and forth on bikes, roller skates, and skateboards, their laughter cracking through the air. And there too was Mrs

Bollard of Number 59, bless her, singing out her hellos to us.

"Well, where ya off to?"

"Off to see a special person," said Da.

"Ah, you're a great one. Never miss a week, do ya? Send her my love," Mrs Bollard said.

Da and I left Derrygreenagh, taking a left out of the Park. Da was a fast walker. For every one of his steps I had to take three. "Come on you," Da shouted back, stopping for a moment, waiting for me, lost in my dreams as usual.

"All truly great thoughts are conceived when walking," Da would say. He was always coming out with these little gems. I caught him up, or at least his shadow, just behind him. I stared at his back, his slim, athletic six-foot frame, large veins pumping from his long, muscular arms. Blue rolled-up sleeve shirt and black trousers, perhaps his only pair. His shoes never looked comfortable, but no one would ever moan about blisters. You put up with what you had. Most of the shoes we had anyway came from St Vincent de Paul, or the English cousins – hand-me-downs for which we were eternally grateful.

Da stopped for a moment, looking up at the sky, then at me. "Y'know, you got your whole life ahead of you," he said, all of a sudden. Then when I was about to say something back he added, "This might be the last of the good weather for a bit. Should've brought a jumper for ya."

"I'll be grand," I said stuffing my hands in my pockets. "Ma says it's hard to kill a bad thing so….". We both laughed, our breath fogging in the chilly air.

I can see my father even now, me ten steps behind. His one swinging arm pointing the way ahead, with the other hand in his pocket. Like a swan, chest out, head held high. I thought that he was the most incredible person.

A horn sounded and a battered old Toyota pulled up. "Jim, I'm only going as far as the Bord," the man coughed through the smoke. "Is that any good for you?"

Da replies, "Ah you're a good lad Mick."

As I jumped into the back of the car I wondered at my father's interaction with chain-smoking Mick. The car seats were torn, yellow sponge poking out. The ashtray was crammed with overflowing cigarette butts. Dried-up air fresheners dangled alongside rosary beads. A blue and white scarf of Waterford hung from the rearview mirror. Mick had black nails and tiny black holes sprinkled across his worn, leathery skin. He had only a few teeth left, but his smile was the kindest you'd ever see.

"Jim, will you have a fag?"

"Ah no Mick, you're grand," Da replied, sucking on his Fisherman's Friend.

"Is this the youngest one, Jim?" I loved to hear a stranger ask my Da about me. As there were so many of us, when he spoke about you there was instant pride to hear yourself spoken of.

"That's Polly, she's the greatest footballer in Ireland." Mick turned around to survey me.

"Ah, Da stop!"

"Sure Jim you were a great footballer yourself."

Mick dropped us off at the Bord na Mona works and we continued on our way. We kept up the chat as we crossed another field, the grass wet. It was easy to believe, in moments like these, that it was just me and Da, alone with the wind rustling through the hedgerows, the only walkers for miles around.

"We'll make a historian out of ya yet," he said, about to launch into another rant about empire. But then he switched again. "Remember, always keep an eye on where you're going, and don't forget the stories of where you've been."

Da grabbed my arm and, hand-in-hand, we crossed the main Dublin-Galway road. We were now on Droichead Chaisleán Loiste, Lost Castle Bridge, and we got to the thumbing point at Rhode – our journey had barely begun at this stage.

"Let me show you where Pat and I made a bridge, right over the field to Granny's house," Da said to get my mind off the 15 kilometres walk to Ballinabrackey. I was excited to see the bridge Da and his brother Pat had put together. Was it going to be as grand as Beggars' Bridge in the village?

"Come on, Da!"

"Ah sure, we're nearly there."

"Not another one of your 'We're Nearly Theres!' Hurry, let's go to the bridge!"

I think we took a different, longer route that time. Da would like long periods of silence, deep in thought. Da's footsteps were heavy. I knew better than to bother him when he got like this. Instead, I watched a squirrel run up a tree, its fluffy tail flicking as it disappeared among the branches. Just then, a rustle in the bush caught my attention, a fox's curious eyes paused to look at us. Da must have seen it too because he stopped and let out a sharp breath. I glanced up at Da, but he said nothing, a faint smile on his lips, sharing something without words. Finally, we reached the back of Granny's field. We stopped at two logs, wedged across the stream, held in place by rope at each end.

"What's that?"

"Isn't it a grand and mighty one?" Da said.

"Hardly. Is that what I came all this way for?" I shrugged. "Da, why did your brothers move to the UK and you stayed in Ireland?"

"Sure who would show you the bridge if I was gone?"

We'd arrived at Granny's. Pippa Heavey was leaping around our ankles as we made our way to the porch at the back. There was another little white gate before we entered through the back door where we met another dog. Prince was ten times the size of Pippa yet ten times quieter. Daddy rang the doorbell and out came Auntie Pauline. Maureen and Veronica were out that day. It was just Pauline and Granny in the house. Granny had been bed-ridden for ten years and was cared for by Da's sisters, so she was mainly confined to her room.

"Ah hello Jim," says Pauline, "how did you get here?"

"Ah sure we walked and got a lift from Mick, you know Mick from Ballinderry, Mick O'Brien?"

"Get in, get in. Will you have a cuppa?" asks Pauline. Taking out the 7Up, she poured me a glass and put the kettle on for Da.

"How's Mother?" Da asked.

"Ah she's keeping well today, sure go down to her," said Pauline, "and I'll make a few sandwiches." The smell of rhubarb tart filled the air, which was all I had on my mind, not saying hello to Granny. We made our way down to Granny's room. The walls were cluttered with family photos, a collage of smiles and memories spanning decades. But all I could think of in that moment was the tart, the rhubarb tart!

We went into Granny's room. Granny lay in a large quilt-covered bed, against an array of pillows. "Ah, there you are!" she says smiling faintly at Da. She hadn't spotted me behind.

Da sat at her bedside, taking her hand. "How are you today, Mother?" he asked.

"Better now, Jim." She spotted me. "Look at her growing taller by the day!"

"Hi, Granny. Da's been telling me stories."

"Oh, the stories he could tell!" she said.

Auntie Pauline came in with a tray of tea and biscuits, setting it on the small table beside Granny's bed. "There we go," she said, pouring us each a cup.

We gathered around, sipping warm tea and nibbling on biscuits. Da bent down and kissed Granny on the forehead. The room smelt of age. Sunlight pressed through thick curtains, casting beams that both illuminated and softened the room's colours. By Granny's bedside were her most treasured possessions: rosary beads perfectly arranged, a small bottle of holy water reflecting the filtered sunlight, and a well-used Bible. A modest spray of red roses by the window breathed life into the room. A single chair was positioned by the bed.

Da filled the air with his usual talk of Meath football, religious gossip, politics and the latest goings-on, while Granny, mostly silent, drifted in and out of our realm. Then Da had a quiet moment with Granny, her hand held in his. When it was my turn, I cherished holding Granny's soft hands.

After another lengthy pause, Granny simply said, "Give my love to all."

Da got up, and we tiptoed out, through the sitting room and down the hall to the kitchen.

"Sit down, sit down!" Pauline offered. "Will ye have your soup?"

The little ham sandwiches were all neatly arranged, and the tea offered in Granny's fancy china set that had been used to serve the Bishop of Meath. And the rhubarb tart! My hands itched to grab a piece, but we always had to give thanks first.

"Bless us with good food, the gift of company, and hearty laughter. May the love and joy we share be with us ever after, Amen."

The time was passing and Pauline didn't have the car to drop us back as Maureen and

Veronica, the other sisters, were using it. "We'd better be off Pauline," Da said.

"Sorry I don't have the car Jim," said Pauline.

"Not a bother. Sure there will be loads going up the road from the Bord. We'll make our way there."

We thanked Pauline again and left, passing Pippa at the porch and Pauline blessing us with holy water, one big splash before we left. Past Prince, through the gate and the manicured garden, roses blooming, green earthy grass freshly cut. "Be careful, God bless you, I'll be up to see you soon."

On our way back we got lucky. Da spotted old Tom Callahan in his red van outside Ballinabrackey. "Tom, you headed our way?" Da asked, his voice carrying the easy familiarity of years known.

"Aye, hop in the back. Got a delivery to make near your place anyway," Tom replied.

Da helped me into the back of the van, filled with sacks of spuds and a couple of crates with chickens. From the window I watched the bog come alive. Machines sliced through the earth, each layer darker and richer than the one before. Da always said that the bog was a sponge and would release pure water. The view was breathtaking, a mosaic of greens and browns, with the bog river gleaming in the distance. Bog cotton swayed in the breeze and the sky was a strange yellow, spitting a light drizzle that made the air sparkle.

"I wouldn't trade this for anything," Da said softly.

Printed in Dunstable, United Kingdom

80104092R00068